AF328422

MABEL NICHOLSON

This book is from a series about Modern Women Artists
published by Eiderdown Books.

Other titles available from the same series:

To order books, please visit eiderdownbooks.com

MABEL NICHOLSON

Lucy Davies

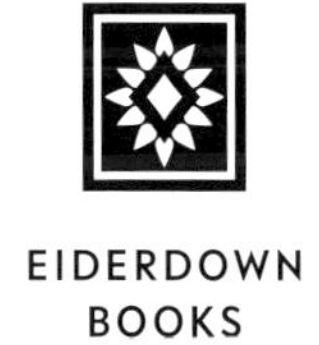

EIDERDOWN
BOOKS

MODERN WOMEN ARTISTS

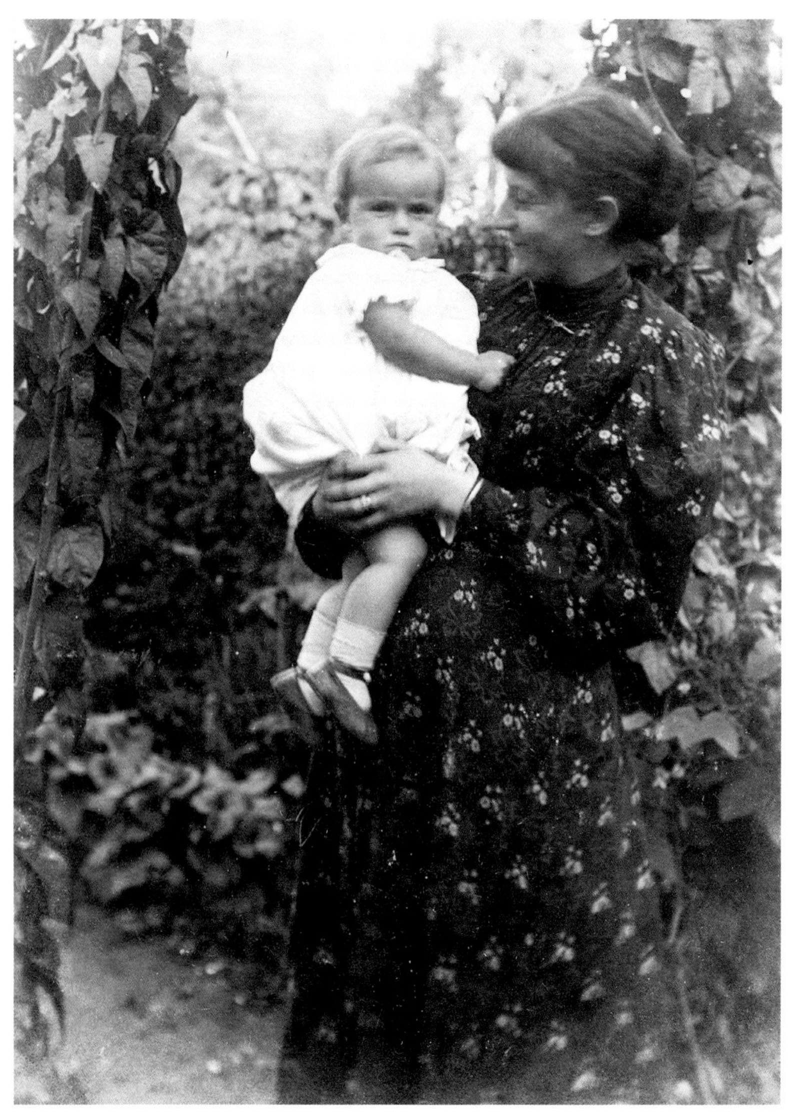

1. Mabel with Ben, c.1896

Few artists win lasting renown without salting away a significantly-sized body of work and Mabel Nicholson (1871-1918), who waited until her four children were grown to paint in earnest and died suddenly at 47, wasn't granted that chance (Fig. 1). Even so, her finest pictures – the figures in Commedia dell'Arte costume; the cryptic, beautifully muted portrait-interiors – all painted in the early 1900s, suggest an artist of such tensile strength that you have to wonder what she might have become.

A born rebel with a resourceful intelligence, Mabel lived through the successive blastings that Parisian 'isms', the Bloomsbury Group and the vorticists brought to late Edwardian Britain, but did not throw her lot in with any of them. Not because her loyalty lay with the desiccated Academic movement – she didn't ally herself with any clear-cut group, in fact – but because her painterly preoccupations were in the field reserved for personal experience; what Walter Sickert described as 'the magic and poetry which [artists] daily see around them.'[1] Her children in particular – Ben, Tony, Nancy and Kit – are viscerally bound into her practice.

Mabel's story slipped from history's grasp amid the blizzard of death brought by the Great War (she died of 'Spanish Flu' in the conflict's final months), and also the artistic successes of the men in her family: her husband William Nicholson (the Edwardian society portraitist and virtuoso still life painter), her sons Ben (the pioneer of British abstraction) and Kit (a modernist architect); perhaps also her brother, James Ferrier Pryde (a once vogueish painter of shadowy interiors).

The difficulty of extracting Mabel from their shadow is compounded by her having left little hard trace of herself, not least by ripping, snipping or scratching her face from a number of photographs in her album (see Fig. 6). In those she left intact, her looks can change from shot to shot. There's a smeared palette, a bundle of letters, almost all to Ben (saved because his personal papers were purchased by the Tate), her paintings of course (around 20 of a possible 46 are currently accounted for), a jumble of reminiscences from those who knew her, questionable opinions from many who didn't. The fullest account of her life was written by William's late-life partner, the novelist Marguerite Steen, who rode roughshod over history in the name of a good story, to present her long-dead rival as nervy, glowering, indolent, spendthrift and insular; William's first marriage as one that, 'left no happy memories behind'.[2]

Some of Ben's biographers have hardly been kinder, one of whom blamed Mabel for his 'insecure personality' – despite his insistence that she was 'the rock on which my whole existence is based'.[3] Her 'purpose and integrity ... was the thing that meant most to me in that home life,' he wrote. 'That and her friendship and the fact she backed me up completely.'[4] Piecing all of this together, then, can feel like gathering the shards of a broken mirror and finding they don't quite fit.

Mabel met William at art school, where she earned some notoriety for devilment ('All the small stories I remember about mother,' said Ben, 'are of her vitality and busting up of conventions.'[5]). Like most women of her time, however, she put aside painting on marriage and when she returned, fit it around her other responsibilities – the social visits and the endless organising of meals, sending her children the books and clothes they requested in letters from school.

Holding those incompatible parts of her in tension, as life went disinterestedly on, felt at many times to her to be practically and psychologically impossible. 'It is such a relief to feel I am free for the moment as I haven't been able to leave the children at all since I came back,' she wrote to Ben in 1914. 'My head is full of little rotten servant worries.'[6] They were close, and her conundrum was not lost on him: in 1949, writing to the collector Marcus Brumwell, he reflected that 'she had the power and purpose and I think the "idea" too but expended all on her family as so many women have done.'[7]

Still, one wouldn't want to deny her the force of her own agency. Mabel knew and socialised with most of the leading English painters and discussed with them the latest developments in avant-garde painting. She also knew their patrons and dealers, many of whom showed her work. In fact, once she did begin, she rose by leaps and bounds to become a painter of curiosity and verve – making 'in depth what she could not attempt in width,'[8] as her son-in-law, the poet Robert Graves put it. Her disappearance from the story of British modernism is thus all the more unjust.

———

Mabel Scott Lauder Pryde was born in February 1871, the youngest child of Dr David Pryde – headmaster of a prestigious girls school in Edinburgh; cherished as wit and raconteur among the gentlemen of the city's Pen and Pencil Club – and his wife Barbara.

'[Mabel's] family on her mother's side came from generations of painters and engravers,'[9] wrote Ben; the uncles of whom Mrs Pryde was said to be most vain (Robert Scott Lauder and James Eckford Lauder, both Royal Scottish Academicians) 'merely an incident'.

Together Isabella, Janet (known as Nettie), Jimmy or Jamie, Fanny, Dora and Mabel formed an 'odd, assertive family,' their household one of 'ceaseless, rattling conversation, argument and the violent expression of violent views'.[10] In search of solitude, Mabel was inclined to sequester herself in the kitchen.

She was closest to Jamie, with whom she shared 'interests and ideas . . . foreign to the rest of the Pryde family,'[11] wrote Ben,

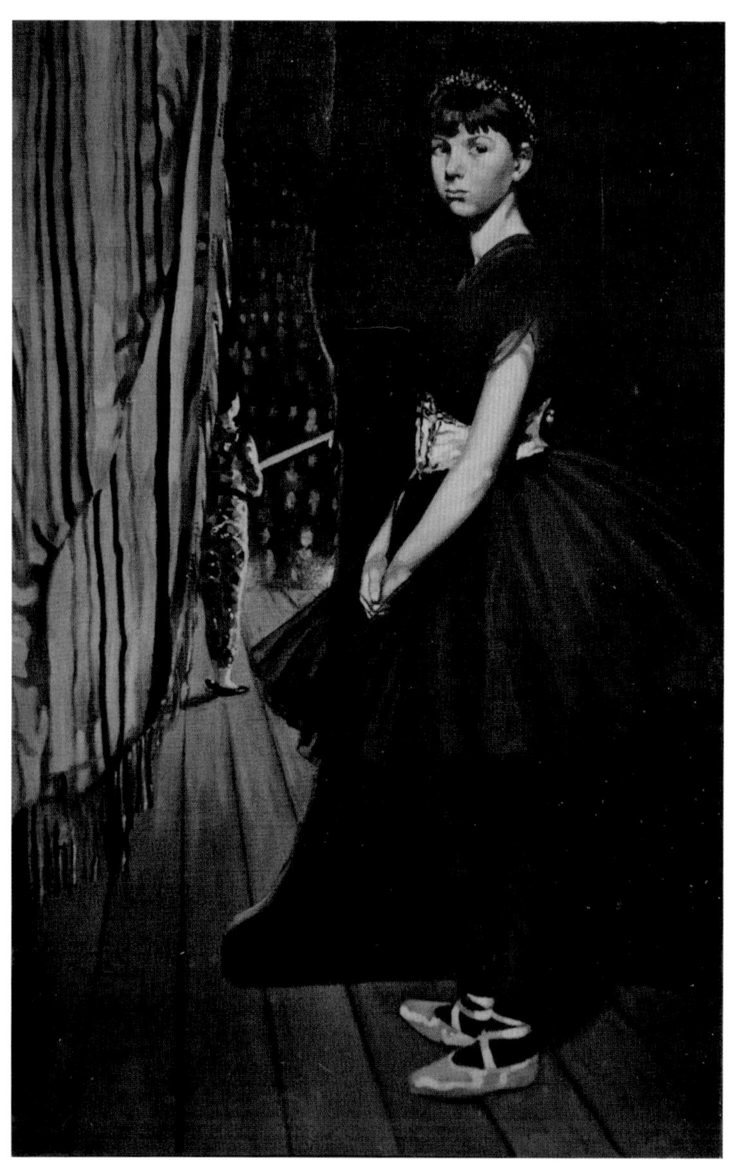

2. Possibly *Columbine*, oil on canvas, exhibited 1911 (untraced)

though all of them were devoted to the theatre. Dr Pryde was a friend of the actors Ellen Terry and Henry Irving, whom he entertained in some style at the Pen and Pencil Club and at home. The cultish frequency with which the Pryde girls attended the Lyceum, meanwhile, raised local eyebrows and Jimmy's habit of dressing as Pierrot lasted well into adulthood.

With this in mind, it is no great surprise to learn that Mabel's paintings later drew on a sense of the theatre as a magical place; the tense atmosphere and smoky chiaroscuro of an auditorium (see Fig. 2). Many also feature costumes – *Columbine*, *Kit as a Pirate*, *The Little Squaw*, *Ben in the Feather Bonnet* and at least three spangle-skinned Harlequins.

The Prydes lived in Edinburgh New Town at 10 Fettes Row, a townhouse of medium size with handsome wrought iron pineapple-finial railings. Today the view from the top floor is blocked by a brutalist (and now derelict) office building, but in Mabel's day it stretched – mist permitting – across the estuary to Fife, where Dr Pryde's ancestors had farmed at Balbedie.

Aged 17, Mabel petitioned her parents to go to the world-renowned, if slightly out-of-the-way School of Art in Bushey, Hertfordshire, run by the German-born Royal Academician Hubert von Herkomer. Students were admitted on the strength of submitted work, eventually progressing to the (segregated, the models in loincloths for the women) Life Class by invitation.

If Mabel had grown restless for a life beyond Edinburgh, then her father was partially responsible: second only to Dr Pryde's enthusiasm for the stage was his belief that the failure to educate girls was 'one of the great calamities of the human race'. His 1200-odd pupils at the Ladies College – among them his daughters – were provided with a rigorous curriculum. He appears in the minutes of the College governors requesting *Macbeth* be introduced into the senior class, 'if divested of all objectionable passages'.[12]

Mabel was Herkomer's youngest girl pupil. Perhaps because of that, or because she once drove a flock of geese into the

Life studio, she came to the attention of the youngest male – William Nicholson. He took to calling her Prydie, while she adopted the nickname bestowed upon him by his closest friends, 'Kid', for his boyish looks (for one photograph, he dressed as a baby). The gesture suggests a charming camaraderie, and certainly, 'these two bright spirits do not appear to have allowed themselves to be unduly weighted down by art,' Steen writes archly, though even she conceded that Mabel was gifted, outclassing 'all the rest put together'.[13]

Mabel's son-in-law Robert Graves later explained how 'it was not that [Mabel] did not recognise the power of the masters, old or new, but that painting, in her mind, was a business that could only concern the actual painter. Her view of life was so uninfluenced and free … Nobody was ever known to move her in any direction against her inclination … and nothing could induce her to work when disinclined.'[14]

Perhaps of more influence, given the theatrical tenor of her paintings, were the elaborate so-called 'pictorial music-plays' that Herkomer and his students presented in the red sandstone cloisters on the school site. He thought of the stage in the manner of a canvas, using electric light and gauze to create a painterly interplay of shadow, form and movement. *An Idyl*, the story of a medieval blacksmith's daughter wooed by a count (she resists!) ran to 13 performances in 1889, and its cast list – printed in *The Hertfordshire Advertiser* on 8 June – includes a 'Miss Pryde'.[15] Herkomer put on a special train from London for a star-studded audience, among whom were Ellen Terry and her son, the future actor and stage designer Edward Gordon Craig, who was so bowled over by Herkomer's carefully lit gauze, with its moving clouds and halo-encircled, paint-and-tissue-paper moon, that he later adapted the artist's methods for his own productions. That Mabel absorbed Herkomer's 'stage picture' ingenuity too is perhaps apparent in the muscular shadows of her 1912 painting *Family Group* (Fig. 16) and in the atmosphere of her portraits, which seem to

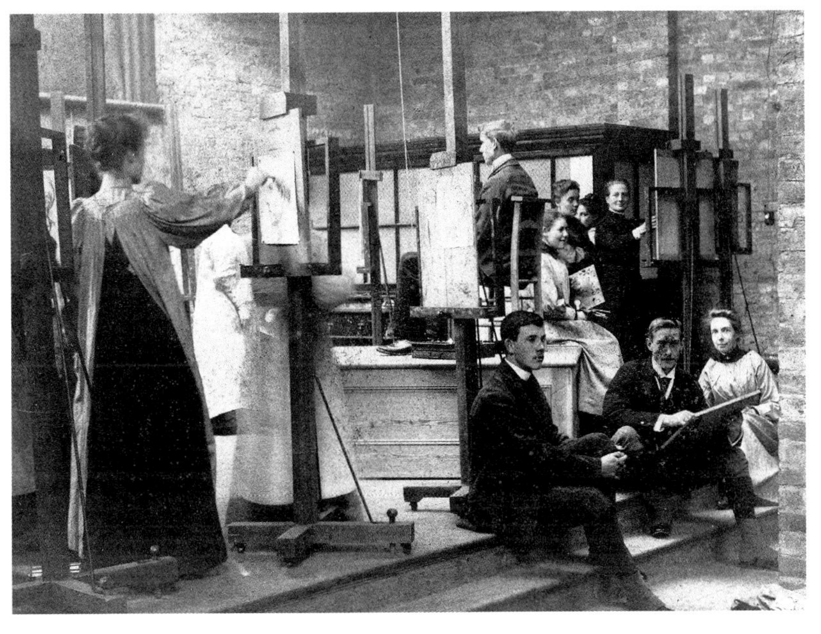

3. Students at Herkomer's School of Art, Bushey, late 1880s,
from an album belonging to James Pryde

turn on their use of what Herkomer described as 'that mystic tone ... which causes forms to become indefinite, and melt together into mere tone'.[16]

Mabel was still in Bushey in 1891, though not officially at Herkomer's school. So many students created their own studios in the village that eventually Herkomer commissioned a series of temporary structures for the purpose and the village effectively became an art colony. William, who had managed to offend Herkomer more than once by, for example, using big brushes, à la Whistler, rather than the fine type Herkomer prescribed, departed for Paris and a stint at the Académie Julian. His and Mabel's alliance continued to flourish, however, and on 25 April 1893, they ran away to Ruislip to be married without their parents' knowledge, honeymooning at Primrose Hill Farm.

Denham and Woodstock

With an allowance of £150 per annum (about £16,000), the Nicholsons began married life in Denham, Buckinghamshire, 'a little one street village of a very few cottages ... and tall trees all around,'[17] recalled Gordon Craig, who lived nearby.

The Eight Bells was a 17th-century cottage and had not all that long ago been an ale house. From time to time a confused customer might knock expecting a glass of beer. Mabel saved one shilling a week, primarily to fund trips to the theatre in London, though Irving often sent her first-night seats. Ben, it is said, narrowly missed being born in the stalls, when she could not be dissuaded from attending Pinero's *The Second Mrs Tanqueray* in April 1894. The Nicholsons would have four children in all: Anthony or 'Tony', in 1897, Annie, always 'Nancy', in 1899 and Christopher, or 'Kit' in 1904.

The two surviving paintings of Mabel by William – very few given his career as a portraitist – date from their time in Denham. It is widely believed[18] she sat for *Lady in Yellow* (Fig. 4), painted the year they married and less a portrait per se than a

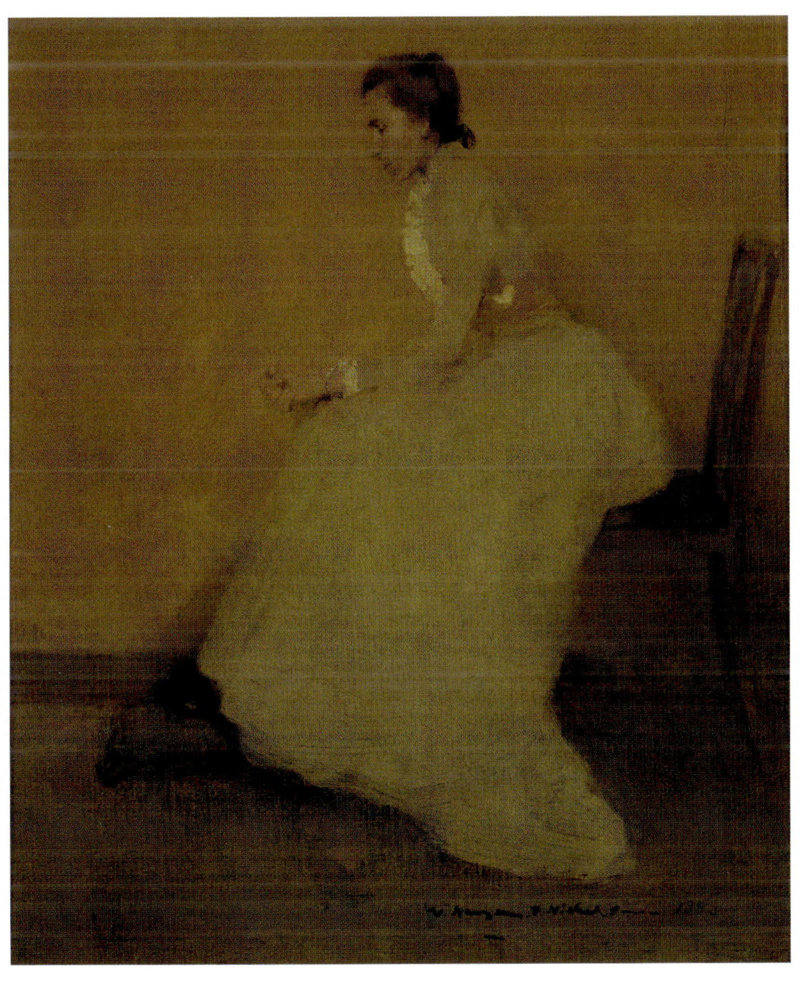

4. William Nicholson, *Lady in Yellow* (Mabel Nicholson), 1893, oil on canvas

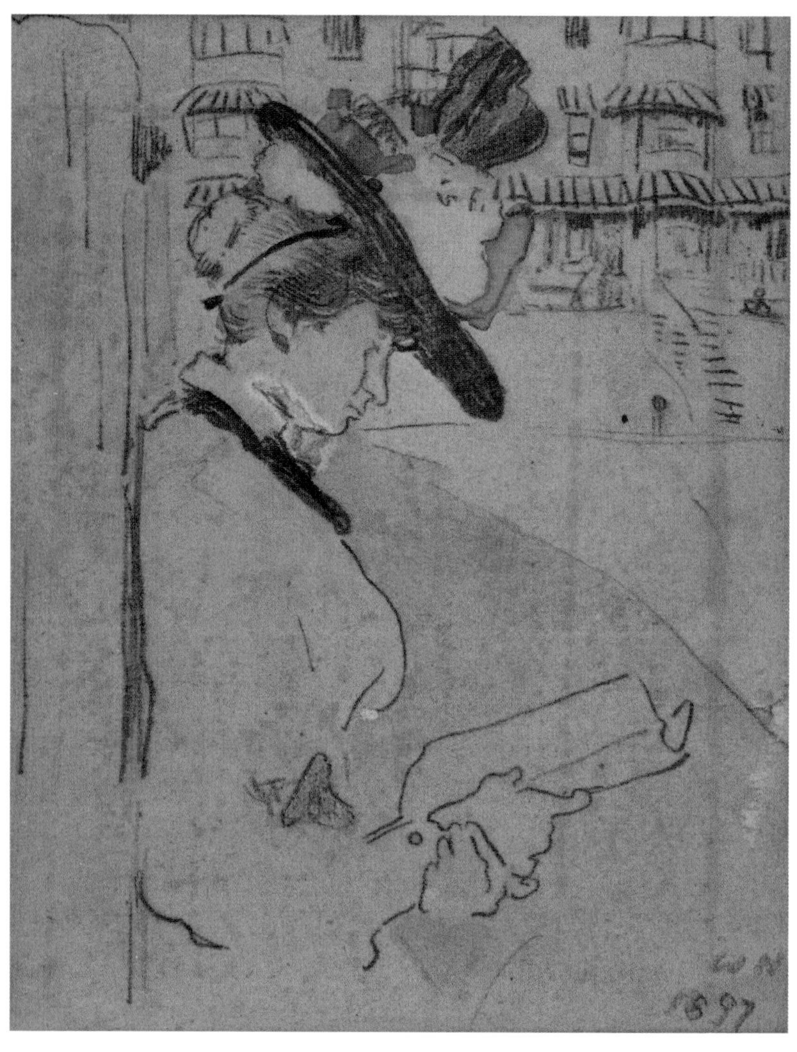

5. William Nicholson, *Portrait of Mabel Nicholson*, 1897,
watercolour and pencil on card

picture on a theme (following Whistler's *Symphony in White* series), but beautiful all the same. The second, a small watercolour and pencil on card dated 1897, captures Mabel intently reading (Fig. 5). It is reminiscent of Henri de Toulouse-Lautrec, whose posters William had seen recently in Paris and greatly admired. The striped canopies behind her suggest a beachfront – likely one of the resorts near Rottingdean in Sussex, where they took lodgings between August and September that year for William to make a woodcut of Rudyard Kipling. In the evenings, Kipling, 'who had taken a fancy to Mabel, used to come round, sit on a black box and tell stories'.[19]

Denham was a giddy time for the Nicholsons. First Jimmy, then Gordon Craig and his wife May moved in, a set-up that proved as vitalising as it was unconventional. William and Jimmy were soon at work on the radical stencil and cut-paper posters they produced between 1894 and 1899 under the pseudonym 'Beggarstaff', while also teaching Gordon Craig wood engraving. 'They live and work together in good comradeship,' observed the *Idler* magazine journalist who came to profile the Beggarstaffs in 1896. 'The whole house is an artist's home from the top to the bottom.'[20] It was a life 'so independent, so very beautiful,' said Gordon Craig: 'Lots of fresh air and sunshine and old Jimmy fast asleep upstairs and the Kid and his active bubbling wit and Mabel and her little Ben in her arms.'[21] William also recalled his wife accompanying herself singing Scottish songs on an old spinet.

In the second volume of her autobiography, published long after William's death, Steen claimed that Mabel and Gordon Craig had an '*affaire*'.[22] Whether this was true – the denouement of their fairly bohemian set-up perhaps – is impossible to know, though Gordon Craig was evidently smitten: a note in his 'day-book' for 9 November 1895 spurred the recollection that: 'An exhibition was on at Olympia which attracted Mable [*sic*] and myself. Mable *was* something; but unfortunately not my wife . . . a remarkable woman.'[23]

In September 1898, with Tony almost one and Mabel heavily pregnant with Nancy, the Nicholsons moved to Woodstock in Oxfordshire. Chaucer's House, opposite the gates of Blenheim Palace, had once belonged to William's mother, Annie Prior.

Mabel's photographs here are a bucolic spread, of children playing at tug-of-war and with hoops; dressed in tam-o-shanters, 'American overalls' and sailor suits; mixed in with souvenir snaps from Hampton Court, on holiday in Dieppe and at Ben's sports day (Figs. 6 and 7). He was sent away to board in 1902, recalling that: 'When seeing me off on the school train she used to remark that on no account must I come back top of my form as boys who did this never did anything afterwards, and doing something with one's life afterwards was what mattered.' [24]

Her letters to him are filled with the salve of mundane goings-on. In May 1903: 'Nancy has cut her fringe off while we were in town and she does look a little fright. The tortoise is getting on and always goes back to sleep at the side of the conservatory. Nancy takes a letter to the post every day for you anointed [?] with a bit of stamp paper on and scribbling.' [25]

If things were not quite stable – in 1899 both of William's parents died; he inherited little and lost his allowance – it was also a time of expansion. He had recently signed a contract with the publisher William Heinemann to produce portfolios of woodcuts, though in 1901 he abandoned them for the more lucrative portrait painting. More importantly, Edwin Lutyens and Max Beerbohm joined their fast-growing circle of sophisticated, bohemian friends.

In all this time, Mabel did not paint – though in 1900, an article about William's woodcuts in *The Magazine of Art* featured a line drawing taken from a pencil sketch of William that is initialled 'MN'. [26]

Graves later wrote that Mabel 'chose to live obscurely', stopping painting 'to concentrate on the welfare of her children', [27] and Steen agreed: 'With the birth of the children, her whole horizon had narrowed to the domestic scene' [28] and 'As each

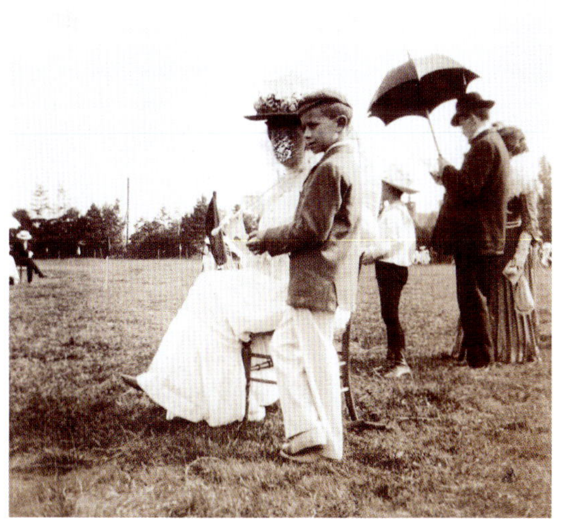

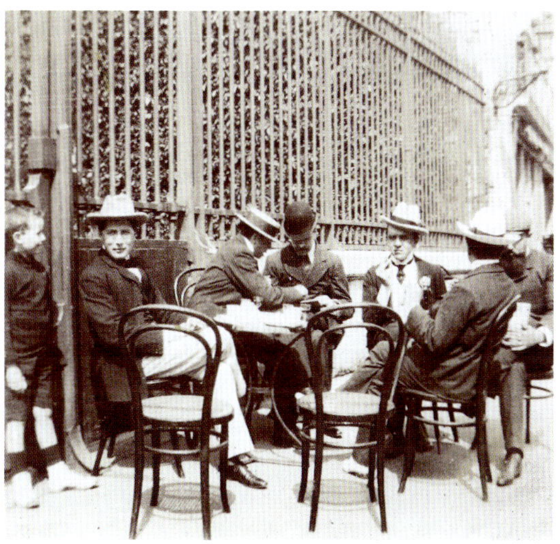

6. Mabel at Ben's school sports day, c.1901, with her face scratched out
7. Ben with Cosmo Gordon Lennox, William Nicholson and
Max Beerbohm, Dieppe, 1903

child appeared she idolised it more than the last. To be separated from them, if only for a day, made her miserable.'[29]

Years after Mabel's death, Steen and William discovered hundreds of letters – now lost – from the children to their mother, tied up in bundles at Apple Tree Yard, the Nicholsons' London home from 1917. 'She must have kept every line [they] ever wrote to her [and] all the letters relating to them: trite notes from nurses, saying that Tony was just cutting a tooth, and Nancy was growing out of her dancing slippers and wanted some new underclothes.'[30]

The incompatibility of motherhood and painting is perhaps a given and feasibly learned from Herkomer, who once dismissed a girl student who had married while enrolled with the advice that her life ought henceforth to be dedicated to the happiness of her husband and children, though in Mabel's case there are signs that something more complicated was involved – her deferral more in the line of foot-dragging, as if she distrusted her own facility.

In 1903, 1905 and 1907, she and William summered in the fashionable resort of Dieppe, on the Normandy coast, with the critic and humorist Max Beerbohm, Reggie Turner, a wit and newspaper columnist, and the actors Marie Tempest and Constance Collier. Mabel's album includes several photographs of the group, children tugging at their ankles. 'These were gay and happy days,' Ben recalled.[31]

The town was a magnet for a varied cultural crowd, but it was swarming with artists, many of whom joined the Nicholsons and their group at the Café des Tribunaux, the Café de Rouen and the hotel Lefevres. Walter Sickert, who had been living in the town since 1898, was one attendee, along with several artists with whom he later formed the Camden Town Group, such as Spencer Gore, Charles Ginner and Albert Rutherston, who recalled meeting William at Lefevres.[32] The Nicholsons also spent time in the home of the French painter Jacques-Emile Blanche – the most sought-after artist of the day and a great supporter of Sickert. Edgar Degas, Giovanni Boldini and John Singer Sargent were at one time or another his regular guests, and he often took fledgling artists under his wing. The seaside terrace of his villa was reportedly often dotted with their easels.

It's quite likely that the intensely artistic atmosphere of the town had a part to play in Mabel's renascence: certainly, at some point between her second and third visits, she finally dusted off her palette.

Bloomsbury

Shortly after William's 1906 debut in the annual *Who's Who*, he and Mabel moved to 'a very sophisticated house' in Mecklenburgh Square, Bloomsbury, London.[33] The area was more up-and-coming than established, with the spark of radical thought floating through its plane trees. Half a mile from Mecklenburgh Square, the nascent Bloomsbury Group were meeting – the autumn the Nicholsons moved in, Virginia Woolf was finishing her first short story, 'Phyllis and Rosamond', about women who, like Mabel, 'cluster in the shade' while 'the male sex . . . strut[s] more prominently across the stage.'

It's tempting to imagine that Virginia and Vanessa passed Mabel on the Bloomsbury pavements, and not at all unlikely she would have encountered the Suffragists. In those febrile years, the area was one of the places in which the movement gathered force.[34] The Women's Freedom League, for instance, was founded in 1907 in nearby Bury Place, and martyr Emily Davison lived moments away on Coram Street. Mecklenburgh Square itself was home to Reform House, where various Suffragist organisations had their HQ. It was certainly present enough in Mabel's life for her then eight- or nine-year-old daughter to chalk 'Votes for Women' above the maid's kitchen sink.[35]

It's also true that, as a theatre-goer, Mabel would have confronted the 'women question' dominating the Edwardian stage. Theatre director and suffragette Edith Craig (sister to Mabel's friend Edward Gordon) wrote that it was 'quite impossible nowadays to produce thoughtful plays written by thoughtful people which do not bear some traces of the influence of the feminist movement'.[36]

Heroines of the so-called New Drama tended to be women whose social and sexual identities challenged acceptable social norms; who were lonely or suffocated and yearned for emancipation. Pinero's *The Second Mrs Tanqueray*, for instance – where Mabel almost gave birth – spun on the truism that while men's promiscuity is condoned, women's isn't, while Henrik Ibsen's heroine Nora – *A Doll's House* had its London premiere in 1899 – accuses her husband of treating her as 'his Doll or dicky bird'.

Certainly, there are signs that Mabel was frustrated. On a 1907 trip to Portofino, for instance, where William had been engaged to paint the Baroness von Hutten, Beerbohm recalled Mabel falling one day into a black mood of 'deepening silence and sallowness as she smoked and smoked without ceasing'.[37]

Mabel's letters and Ben's recollections also suggest that she might have sought refuge in domesticity, more so than was required, and felt alienated from the art world in which she more properly belonged. She once told Ben that 'the two rooms she always liked best in any home were the nursery and the kitchen' – a statement he felt compelled to qualify with 'studio not mentioned I think because she never had a proper studio of her own until at last she made some money of her own and built one.'[38] And that: 'After a lot of art talk from our visitors she always said that it made her want to go downstairs and scrub the kitchen table. That was more extraordinary than it sounds today . . . the kitchen was a real Edwardian affair, with servants who had to be got out of the way.'[39]

The image made a deep impression on him, appearing over and over again in letters and articles he wrote about his childhood, either to illustrate his artistic antipathy towards anything overwrought – in a 1943 letter to curator Hartley Ramsden on the subject, for instance, he illustrates his point

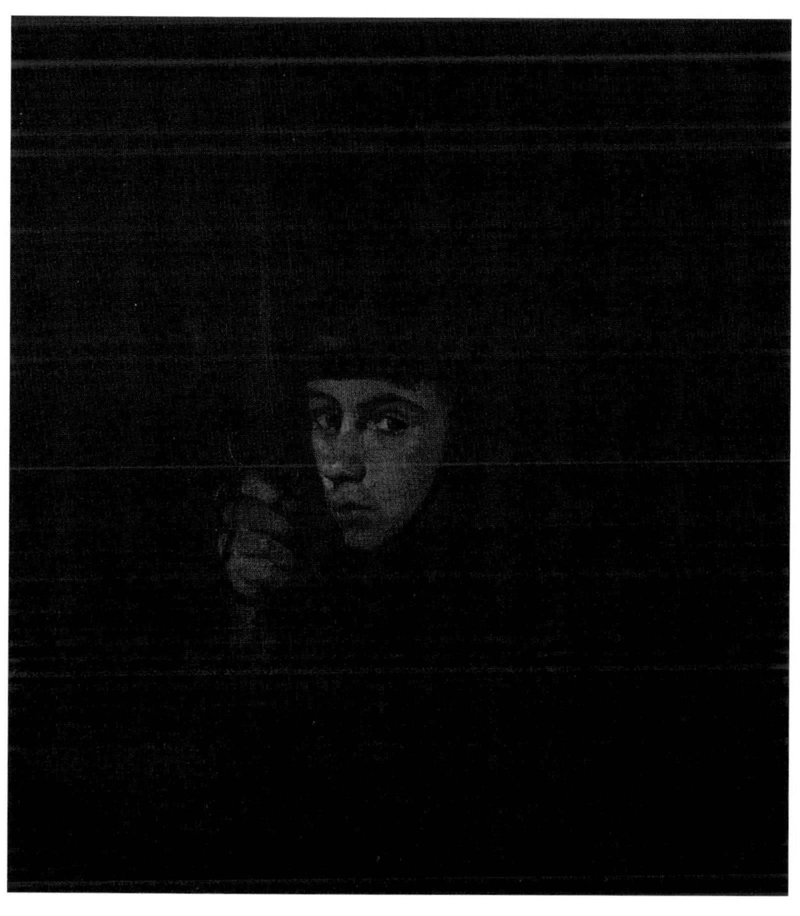

8. *Ben in the Feather Bonnet*, c.1908, oil on canvas

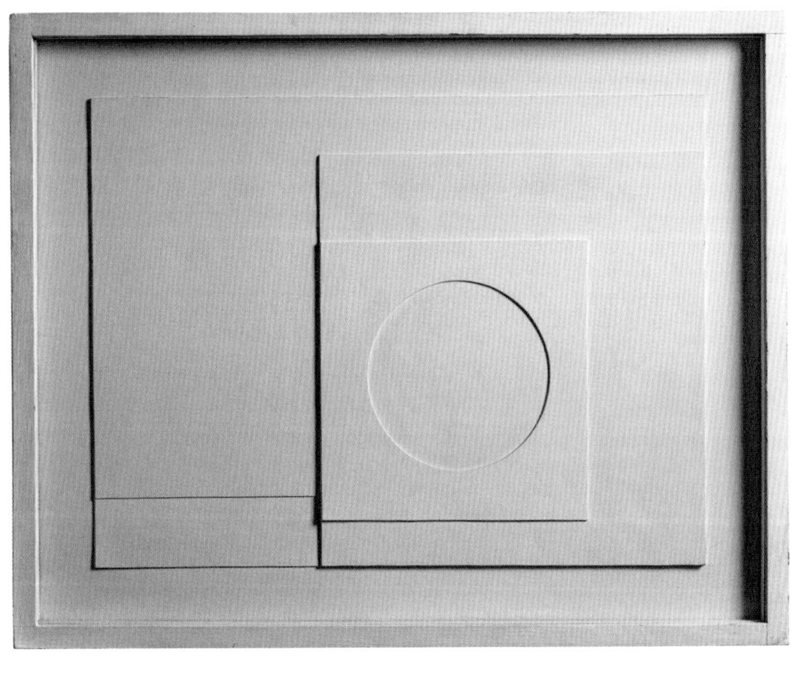

9. Ben Nicholson, 1936 (white relief), 1936, oil on pencil on carved board

with a description of Mabel scrubbing a table 'from side to side & around & into the corners & backwards & forwards'[40] – but also to speculate on the origin of his work. To the art historian John Summerson in 1944 he mused that the action of scrubbing was 'close to marking something rather than painting something ... not unlike ... one of my textured still lifes?' (Fig. 9), and admired his mother's 'anti-swagger ... for although she also was sophisticated, I think this was on the surface and that her nature wasn't at all.'[41]

Both his and William's biographers have suggested that Mabel diverted her artistic frustration into frequent house moves and interior decorating. Whether that is true or not – unequivocally the moves suggest a restlessness but the reality is surely more nuanced, not least because it enriched William's painting to move around – she was tremendously good at it. The drawing room at Mecklenburgh Square featured a black satin sofa, a deep blue ceiling and dragon carpet in bright colours, 'for the time, an extraordinary scheme,' writes Stephen Calloway in his history of 20th-century decoration.[42] It also left a powerful impression on Ben's friend and fellow student at the Slade, Paul Nash, who admired: 'tall mirrors of black plate – gay spotted chintzes ... cunningly matched colours, a severe, aristocratic taste.'[43]

But allowance ought also to be made for the design being a joint project: we know that William painted the panelling at Chaucer House white, for instance, and that he later introduced unusual decorative flourishes at Apple Tree Yard, and hand-laid a Vermeer-style chequered floor in almost every house they occupied.

'Decoration was in the air,' wrote Osbert Sitwell of those pre-First World War years, 'many busied themselves with it ... Every chair-cover, every lamp-shade, every cushion reflected the Russian Ballet, the Grecian or Oriental visions of Bakst and Benois, or else the vulgar and colossal coloured fantasies of Reinhardt.'[44]

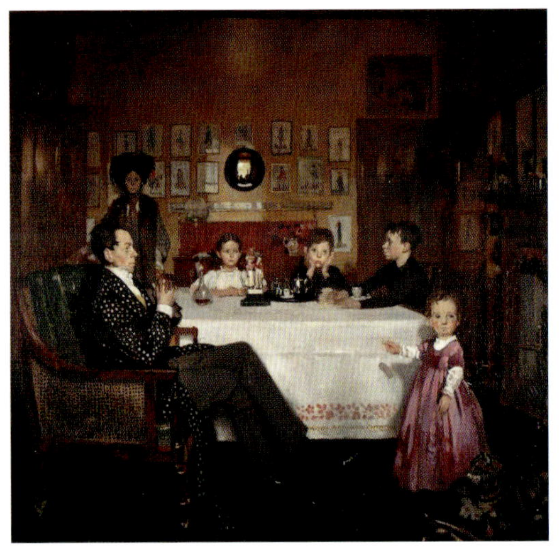

10. William Orpen, *A Bloomsbury Family*, 1907, oil on canvas

Using one's home to project a calculated artistic identity, anyway, was hardly unusual, if not actively required when part of that home was used as a portrait studio, as Nicholson's then was. Both Rossetti and Whistler studded their homes with outré objects designed to register as 'exotic, orientalising, aesthetic, and cosmopolitan' and signal themselves as alternative to the mainstream.[45]

We can see the breakfast room for ourselves – egg yolk walls, black floor, every inch aglow with glass, gilt, boot polish, silk – in William Orpen's 1907 painting *A Bloomsbury Family* (Fig. 10). In the foreground, William presides over sweetly startled and watchful children. Mabel, fashionable in a fur stole, feathered hat and necktie, is standing at the rear. Ben once referred to her 'usual, sphinx-like look' and here it is.[46]

In 1967, Nancy wrote angrily to the art historian Alan Bowness, objecting to an essay in which he had referred to Mabel 'standing in the wings again' in this painting.[47] Suggesting her mother was 'the little wife in the background,' she said, would have made her father squirm. '[He] was not a small person who needed this – and mother was someone to be reckoned with! . . . You can see that it was largely a joke! Father *posed* and mother refusing to sit for him.'

Reluctance to sit would also explain the dearth of paintings of Mabel by William, and perhaps too the wilful self-effacements in her photograph album, which are annotated here and there with William's pencillings: 'Torn out by Prydie of course'. Her position at the back of the room though, might simply have been for composition's sake: in one sketch,[48] Mabel is on the right, and we feel the lack of the upright that her figure provides in the final painting.

William Orpen and his wife had been introduced to the Nicholsons by Beerbohm in Dieppe in 1903, and 'were for a long time very good friends and constantly went about together,' Ben recalled. Moreover that 'whenever Grace Orpen and my mother got together they became completely wild.'[49]

In 1908, the two families holidayed in Margate, where, sat on a rock one evening, the men spied their wives 'far out to sea in full evening dress almost up to their necks (and as my father remarked, my mother was in a new Paquin model as yet unpaid for).'[50] Steen also describes a Georgian costume ball in Covent Garden that ended back at Mecklenburgh Square with Mabel playing the pianola in Persian dress, and Grace 'pulling off her crinoline and dancing like a mad thing in her petticoat'.[51] The crinoline had been borrowed from the Nicholsons' precious chest of costumes, very likely the same one as in *Kit as a Child with Harlequin Clothes*, the picture that seems to mark Mabel's return to painting around 1905 or 1906 (Fig. 11). Its loose, unpretentious style – brushstrokes left visible, the lovely disorder at the painting's middle – suggests it documents a day when circumstance, mood and the urge to paint suddenly aligned, and so she simply set Kit on the floor and began, her instinct for it ready and waiting, even after the long hiatus.

In his catalogue to the 2011 exhibition *The Edwardians* at The Fine Art Society, Professor Kenneth McConkey writes of the painting that: 'Piling up studio impedimenta into a large, jumbled still-life provided an instant test-piece for the nineteenth-century painter, which Mabel Pryde's *Kit with Harlequin Clothes* in essence revives. It was a *genre* that might typically include an exotic costume, a sword or piece armour, a lay figure or statuette, and maybe, a discarded hat. The purpose of this *"chaos décoratif"* was to demonstrate the painter's abilities to prospective clients. It was a kind of badge or shop-sign.'

The harlequin costume captivated her. Around 1908, Nancy posed in it for *Harlequin with Chair*, and again in 1910 for *The Artist's Daughter Dressed as Pierrot* (included in the 1995 survey of Impressionism in Britain at the Barbican). Harlequins also appear in *Columbine* (exhibited 1911, now lost) and *Harlequin Asleep,* c. 1910, though pick of the lot is undoubtedly *The Harlequin* (Fig. 12), Nancy glimmering from the black, almost spectral.

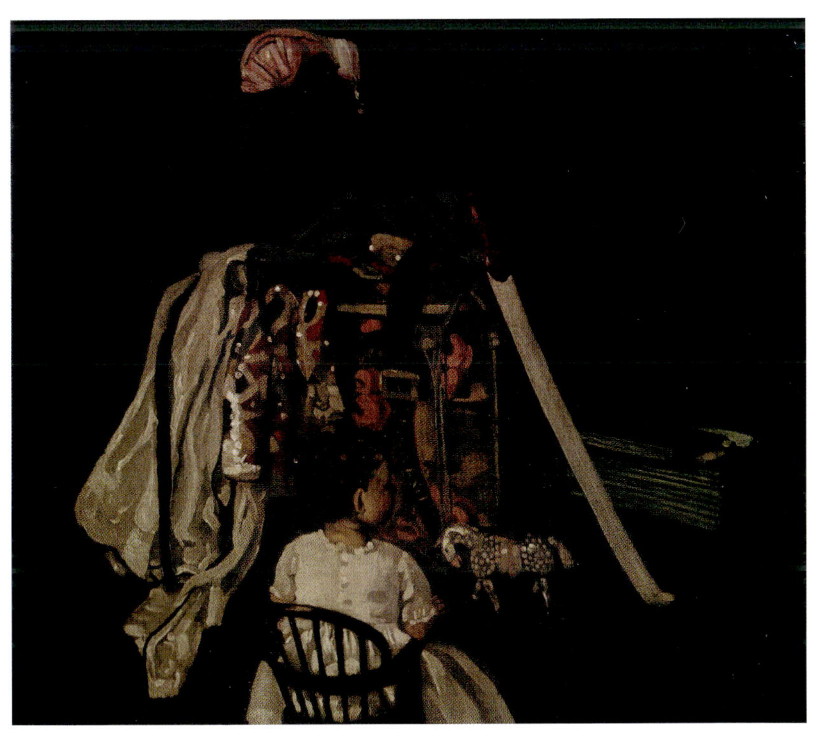

11. *Kit as a Child with Harlequin Clothes*, c.1905, oil on canvas

The use of a solid monochrome background echoes Manet, who was in turn emulating Velazquez – particularly the Spaniard's 1635 *Portrait of Pablo de Valladolid*. 'The background disappears: it is air which surrounds the fellow, dressed all in black and full of life,' Manet wrote to his friend Henri Fantin-Latour.[52] The influence of the great Spanish Caravaggesque masters of the seventeenth century on Mabel and William's circle was 'profound,' writes McConkey: 'It would therefore be easy to ascribe Mabel Pryde's *hispagnolisme* to her brother, her husband and her husband's friends, William Orpen and William Rothenstein, were it not for the suave handling of the harlequin pictures. These in their way are as daring and reductive as Nicholson's landscapes at Rottingdean.'[53]

The harlequin costume could be the one for which Mabel thanked her friend, the collector and gallerist Hugh Lane, in an undated letter written on Mecklenburgh-headed paper[54] – 'It is quite lovely,' she writes, 'and is such a perfect colour to paint.'[55] The Nicholsons and he were close: the reverse of a 1909 sketch by William Orpen depicts the heads and shoulders of himself, Grace, William, Mabel and Lane beside their scores for 'Flying Patience' at the Orpen's home. Mabel's win suggests her talents extended to cards too.

By 1908, she is 'working hard'.[56] Her painting of Ben in an 18th-century Scottish military bonnet is thought to date from this year. It was praised in the *Country Life* review of Mabel's memorial exhibition in 1920 for its 'bold Rembrandtesque allure'[57], and no wonder: though pictorially it boils down to just his steady gaze in the darkness, there it all is – her tenderness, his adolescent uncertainty, the electricity snapping away between them.

The Dutch painter's reputation as an artistic genius was positively cultish in Mabel's time. Exhibitions of his work at the Royal Academy and the British Museum in 1899 were both so

12. *The Harlequin*, c.1910, oil on canvas

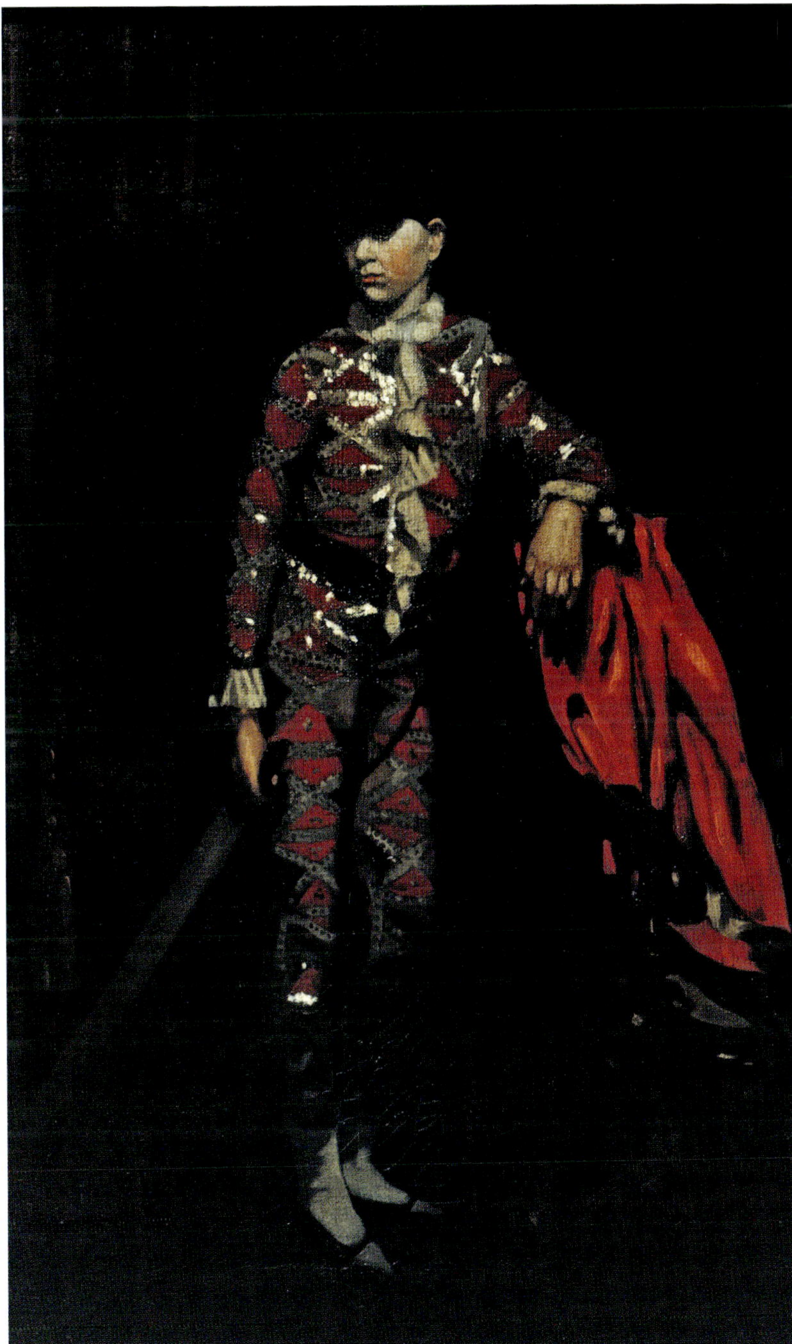

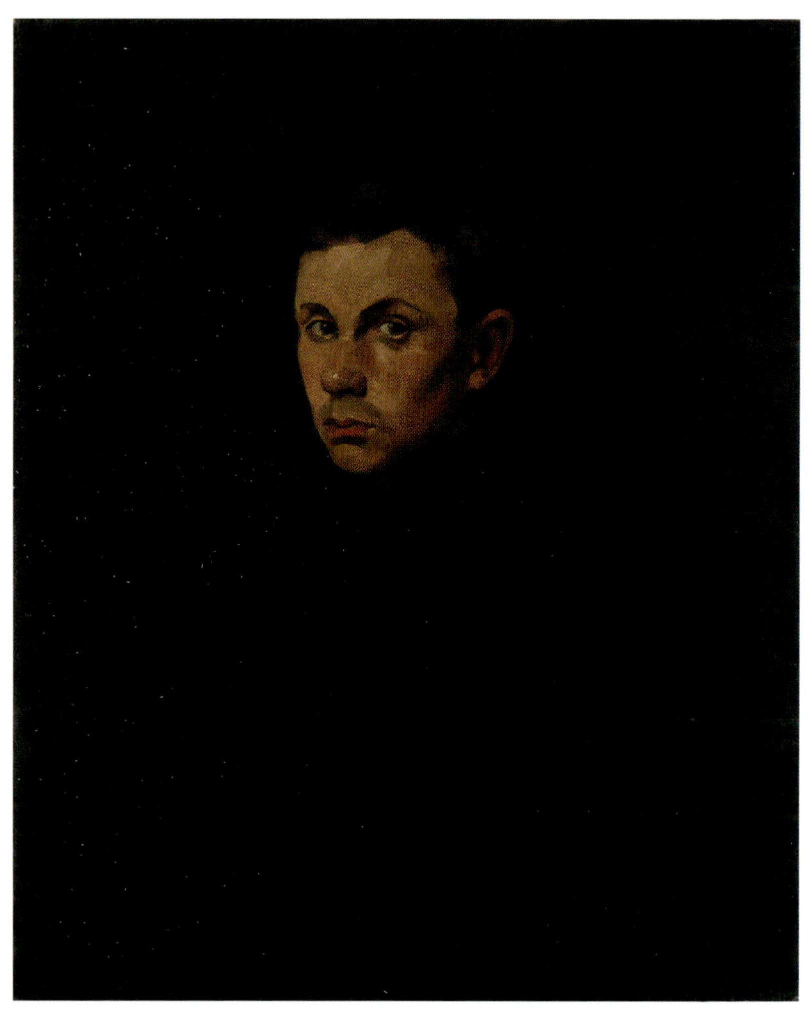

13. Ben Nicholson c.1910–1914, oil on canvas

crammed with viewers that you were hard-pressed to see a picture at all. 'I went to the Rembrandt show which almost takes one's breath away it is so marvellous,' wrote Mabel's Dieppe friend Albert Rutherston to his parents. 'Of course I shall go again.'[58]

Between 1910-1914, she made a second version of the painting (Fig.13). No costume this time, so we focus more intently on his face; its ruby lip, brow and philtrum painted with eloquent precision. Steen observed that Mabel somehow separated her artist self from her maternal self when painting: 'There is no delicacy of fancy,' she wrote, 'but a hard, uncompromising truth which is redeemed through its honesty.'[59]

Rottingdean

In 1909, William and Mabel bought an old vicarage on the Sussex coast – 'a mad thing for a man to do,'[60] William admitted to his patron T.W. Bacon, leaving him £200 in debt and 'in the curiously rotten position of having more houses than food'.[61]

But The Grange at Rottingdean, with its salt wind and crumbling chalk cliffs, was irresistible. 'It is on the downs and 5 minutes from the sea,' Mabel wrote excitedly to Ben. 'It has got a tennis court . . . a small billiard table and plenty of room so I think you will love it.'

The Grange was a beautiful house. Ben's friend, the artist Paul Nash, who came to stay in 1911, remembered it as 'very bright and shiny – highly polished painted walls, stiff calendered chintzes, gay pink and greys.'[62]

Whatever the magic Rottingdean worked on William (the still lifes and landscapes he made here are deemed his best work), it did the same for Mabel. She positively ignited, painting suddenly 'with an ease and certainty hair-raising to William.'[63] Two of her finest paintings date from these years – *The Grange* (Fig. 14), a double portrait of Nancy and Kit in a recessing, stage set-like interior, and *Family Group* (Fig. 16), a subtly disquieting conversation piece featuring Tony, Nancy, Kit and the family nanny beneath a large model ship.

Both respond to the era's vogue for portrait-interior paintings – essentially unposed figures in ordinary rooms, lost in contemplation or a task. Vermeer is its obvious forerunner, but among Mabel's circle Whistler's *Arrangement in Grey and Black No.1* (1871), and Orpen's 1900 painting *The Mirror* are good examples, as is most of Vuillard and Bonnard's oeuvre. Also the Danish artist Vilhelm Hammershøi – who spent time in London at the turn of the century and whose trip to Paris in 1891 coincided with William's.

Mabel added an imaginative inflection of her own, however. *Family Group, Kit in the Glass with Nancy and Sammy* (Fig. 17) and *Kit on the Platform* (Fig. 19) are anything but straightforward depictions of reality. Each has a strangely ominous note humming at its core; one that, the more you look, the more compelling it becomes to try and resolve.

In the case of *Family Group*, much comes from the ship and its long-fingered shadow, a fully rigged and planked model of the Royal Naval frigate Pandora which in 1790 tracked down the Bounty mutineers at Tahiti. Bought in an Edinburgh curio-shop in the mid 1900s (possibly 1905-1906, when William experimented briefly with shipping scenes[64]), by 1911, it was resident at The Grange. Actors Lady Tree and Mrs Patrick Campbell brought an entourage down from London to admire it.

In 1912, the painting was exhibited at both the Goupil Gallery 'Salon' (Goupil were leading West End dealers) and the International Society (a forum for independents – its first presidents were Whistler and Rodin). Mabel had been successfully submitting to the latter for two years by then, likewise the New English Art Club (set up in direct opposition to the Royal Academy – Sargent, Sickert and Beerbohm were members).

In the years leading up to the Great War, the London art world was crammed with these informal, rebellious and increasingly rival groupings. Osbert Sitwell recalled that 'a ferment such as

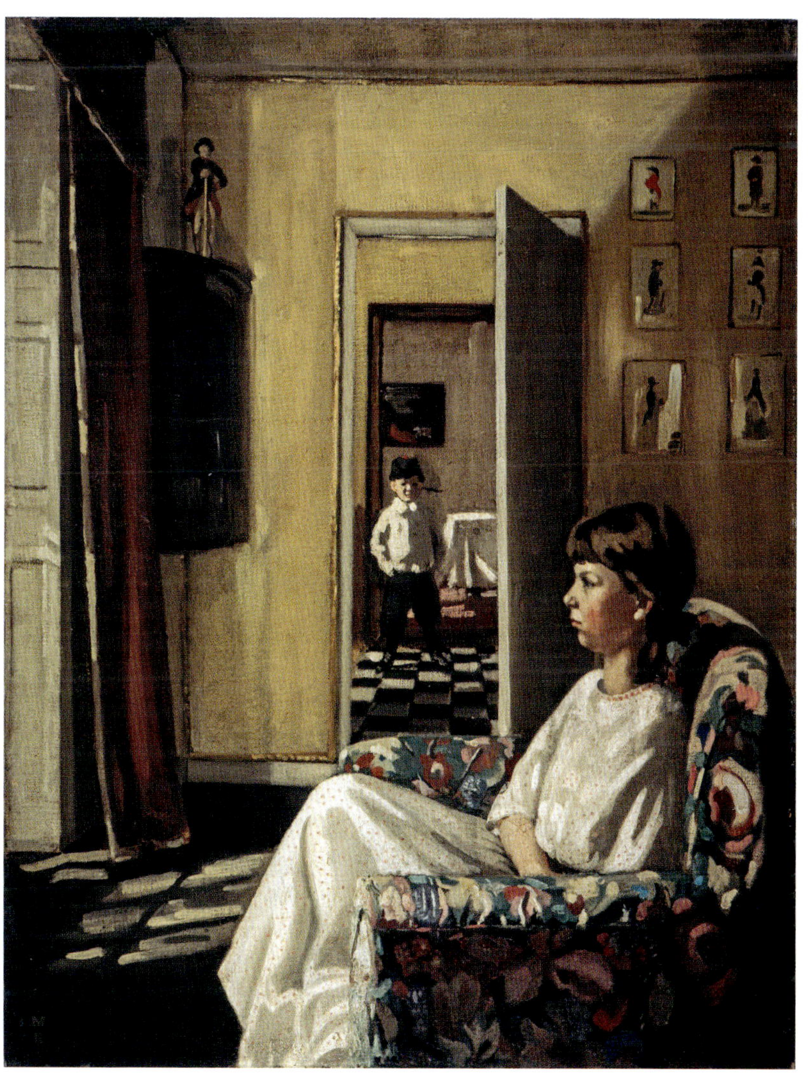

14. *The Grange*, 1911, oil on canvas

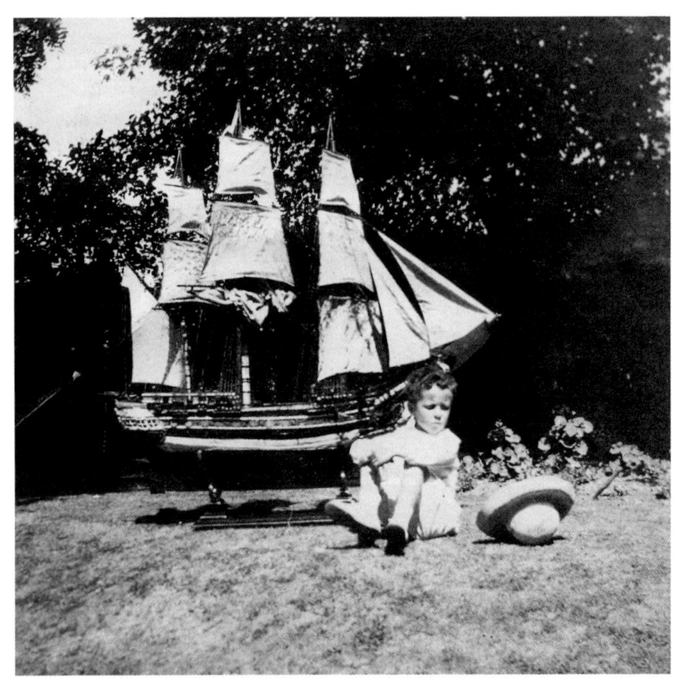

15. Kit with the model of HMS Pandora in the
garden of The Grange, c.1911

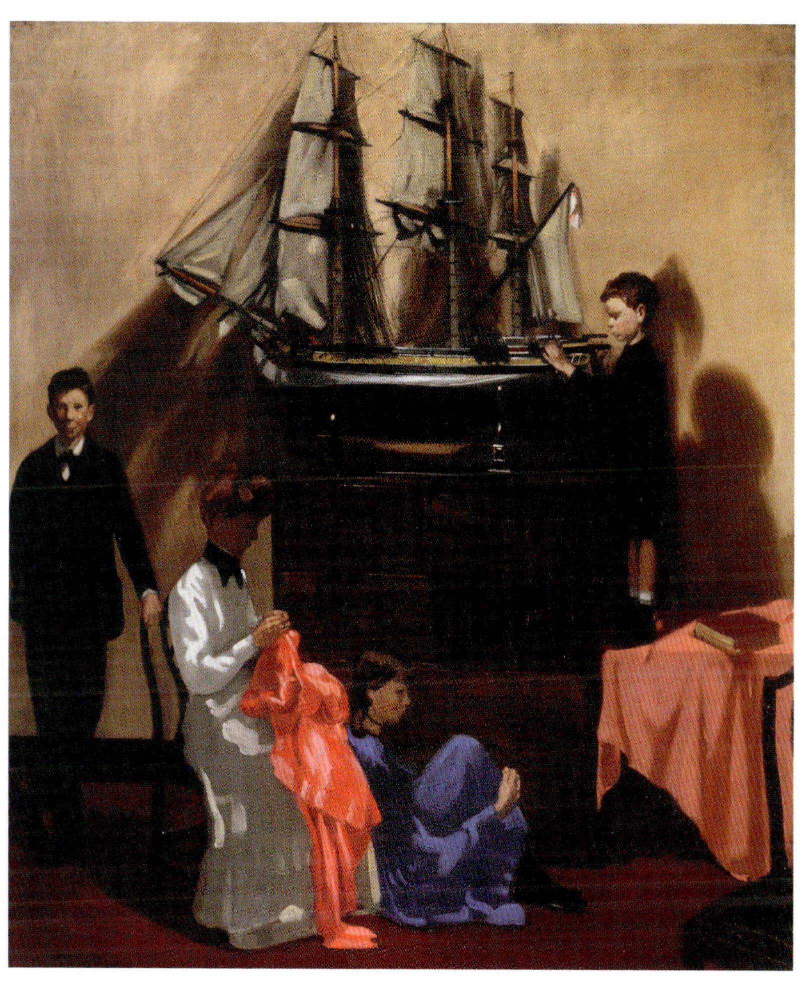

16. *Family Group*, c.1911, oil on canvas

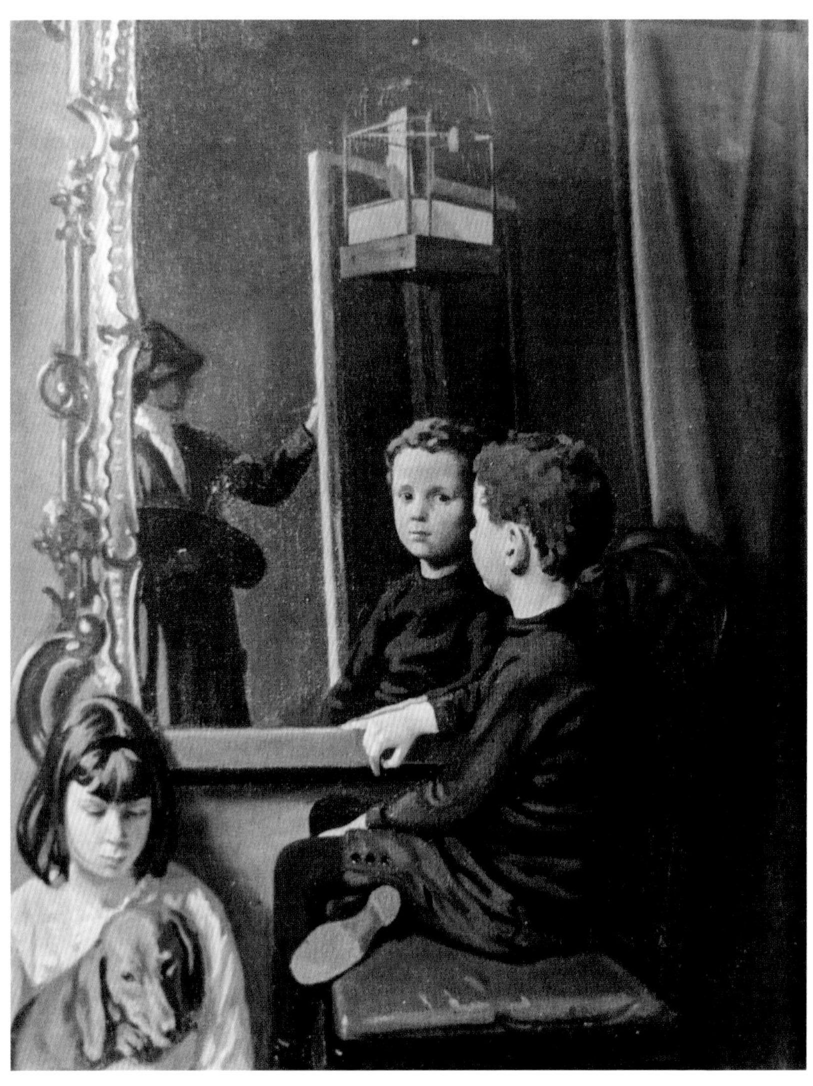

17. *Kit in the Glass with Nancy and Sammy*, showing MN
in the mirror, exhibited 1912 (untraced)

I have since never felt in this country prevailed . . . we possessed again artists of a kind new to us, in whose work showed the national qualities, and who were not merely the imitators of Paris goods.'[65] Mayfair's position as centre of the art world had also begun to teeter: 'Chelsea likes it,' said *The Times* in 1910, 'and Chelsea sets the tone in modern English art.'[66]

It was a coup, then, for Mabel to secure a solo show at the Chenil Gallery in 1912. The picturesque little space on the King's Road was then enjoying its 'greatest critical and financial success'.[67] Augustus John, Ambrose McEvoy and Orpen were also on its roster.

'I have just got my exhibition hung,' Mabel wrote that summer to Ben, 'and must write and tell you that I have sold my big picture of *Kit in the Glass with Nancy and Sammy*[68] for £200 – hooray – isn't it nice, I'm so excited and pleased . . . Lady Cowdray bought it.'

Fired up, she dashed off a similar note to Max Beerbohm: 'I've been working so hard . . . I sold my biggest picture directly I had finished hanging for £200, isn't it wonderful? . . . I can't resist writing to tell you, for I know you (nice, just person) will be pleased.'[69]

The picture is lost, but a black-and-white photograph in the album of Mabel's paintings Ben compiled in 1920 confirms it as her finest work: a tumble of scale and reflections held in tension by Kit's face, the sole of his shoe, his little finger resting on the gilt frame (Fig. 17). That Mabel included herself feels important too: Brush raised, face turned to the easel, first and foremost an artist. Someone worth acknowledging.

With her earnings (it equates to nearly £20,000[70]) Mabel commissioned from Lutyens a thatched studio in the rear garden of The Grange. She and William shared the space (its large north-facing window is recognisable in some of his paintings[71]) though a letter Mabel wrote to Ben in 1914 suggests his need took precedence. Ben also observed to Summerson that the studio 'was so much better than the one father worked in

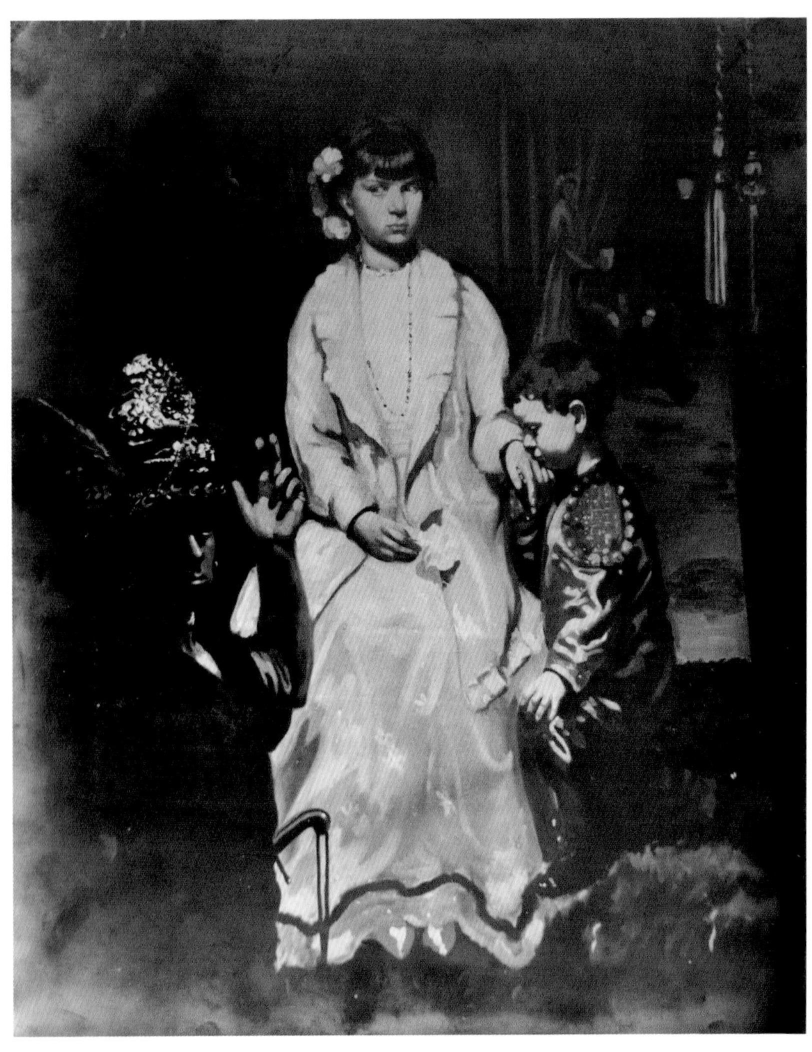

18. Possibly *The Pink Dress*, exhibited 1915 (untraced)

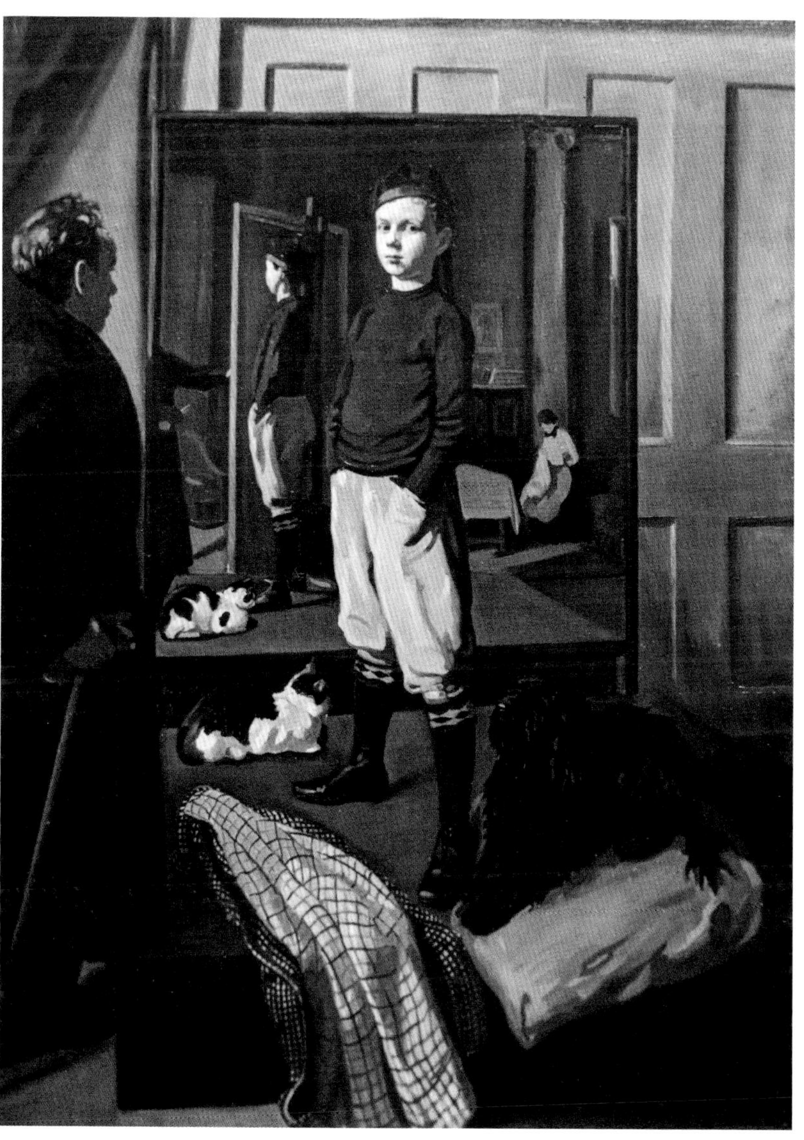

19. *Kit on the Platform*, c.1915, oil on canvas, showing William
on the left and Mabel in the mirror (untraced)

that he quickly annexed it on the plea of urgency in earning money (it occurs in M Steen's version as the studio mother built for father!!).'[72]

Almost without exception (her 1911/12 portrait of William in Regency costume (Fig. 20), and of the locals while with Ben and Kit in Madeira for several weeks in 1913 – *Ernesto, Portuguese Girl* (Figs. 21 and 22)) Mabel painted the familiar faces of her children, and insisted she pay them a fee. As subjects go, she was fortunate. 'I am so glad you like the Nicholson troupe,' wrote Max Beerbohm to artist William Rothenstein in 1911: 'They *are* somehow more like a troupe than a family – Nancy standing with one spangled foot on Nicholson's head, Ben and Tony branching out on tip-toes from his straddled legs, Mabel herself standing at the wings, holding the overcoats.'[73]

The image conjures so succinctly her shared self; an artist in the midst of family life, navigating what American poet Sarah Ruhl described as the 'great systole and diastole of work and children'.[74]

Society portraits remained William's bread and butter. For sittings and to secure commissions, he often travelled to London from Sussex, and leased a studio with living accommodation for the purpose in The Pheasantry, Chelsea. The arrangement secured him not just the isolation and quiet he needed to work, but a mistress.

Marie Laquelle, a French-speaking German, sat for William's 1909 painting *The Girl with the Tattered Glove*, and 1911's *Déjeuner de Marie*. 'Her falling in love with [William] was her mistake,' said Steen, spikily. 'She remained devoted to him for over 30 years.'[75]

Presumably Mabel wasn't immediately aware: in May 1910, writing to Max Beerbohm to congratulate him on his marriage, she said: 'I hope you will be as happy as we are, which is the best I can wish as the Kid gets dearer and sweeter every day.'[76]

Or, perhaps she was – William Orpen, Edwin Lutyens and Edward Gordon Craig were openly well accomplished in that

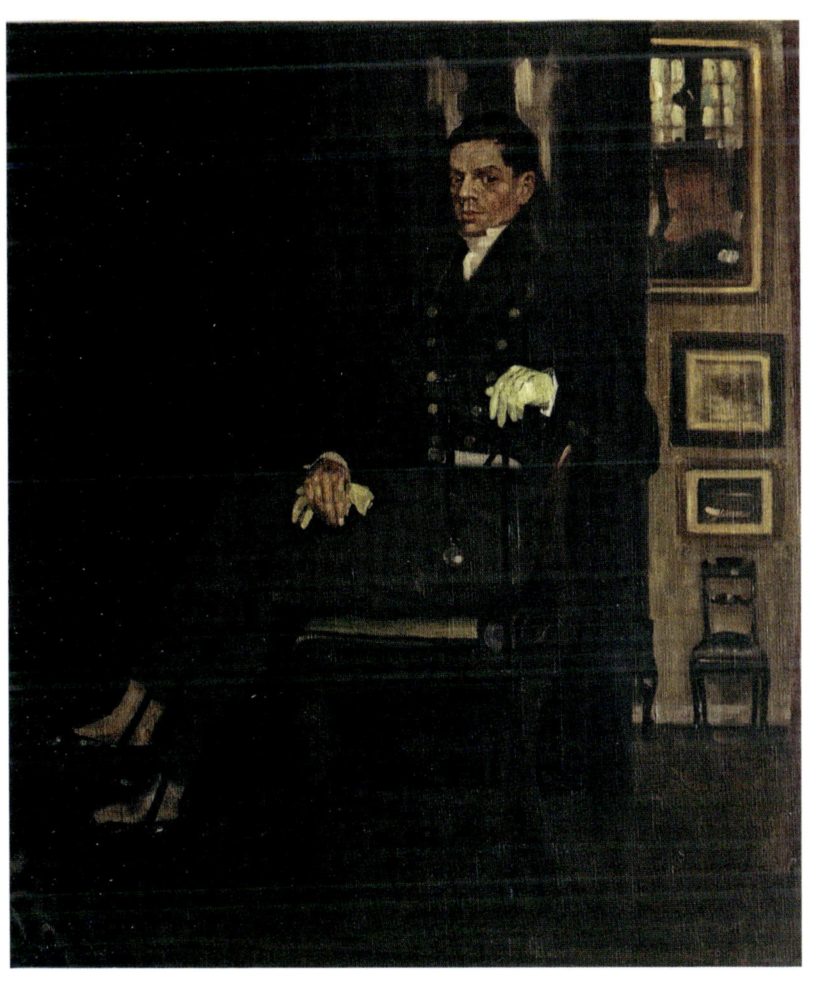

20. William Nicholson, c.1911/12, oil on canvas

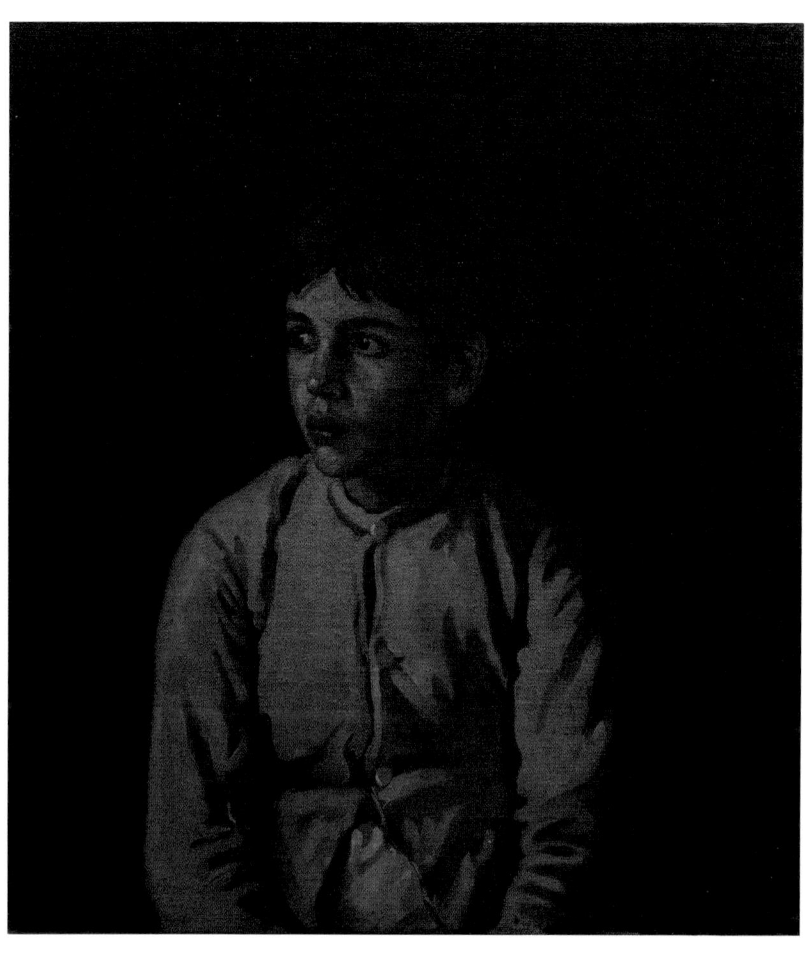

21. *Ernesto (Portuguese Boy)*, c.1913, oil on canvas

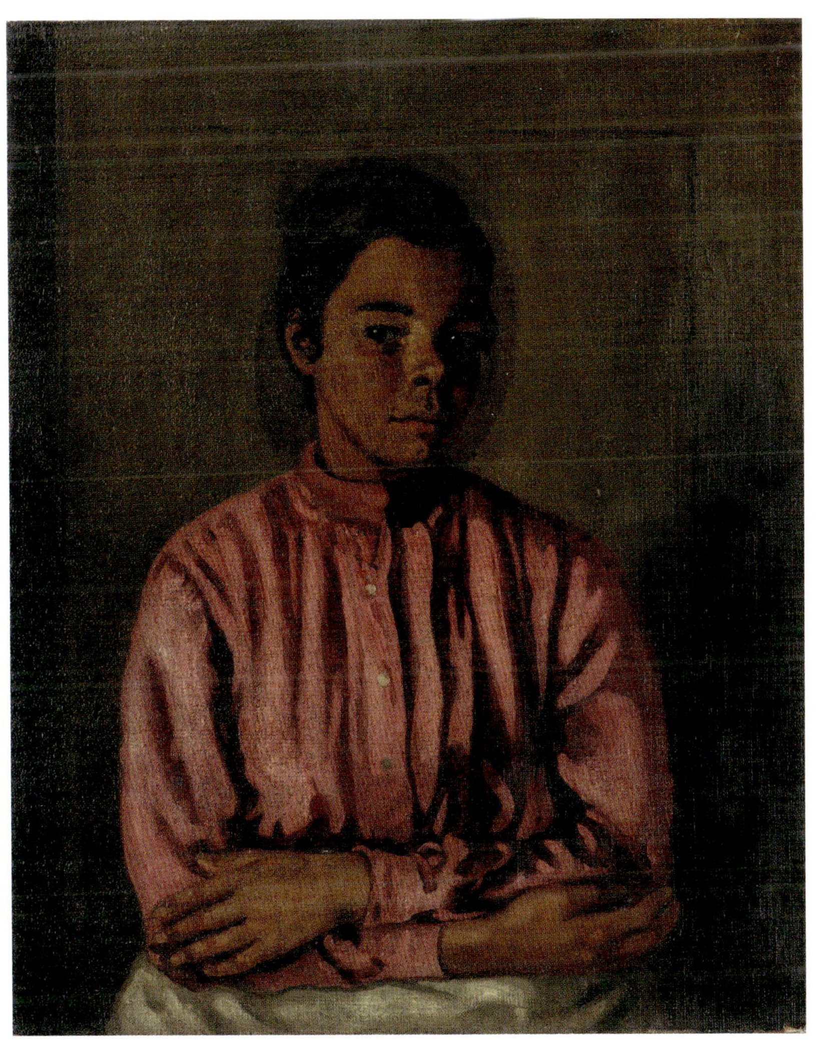

22. *A Portuguese Girl*, 1913, oil on canvas

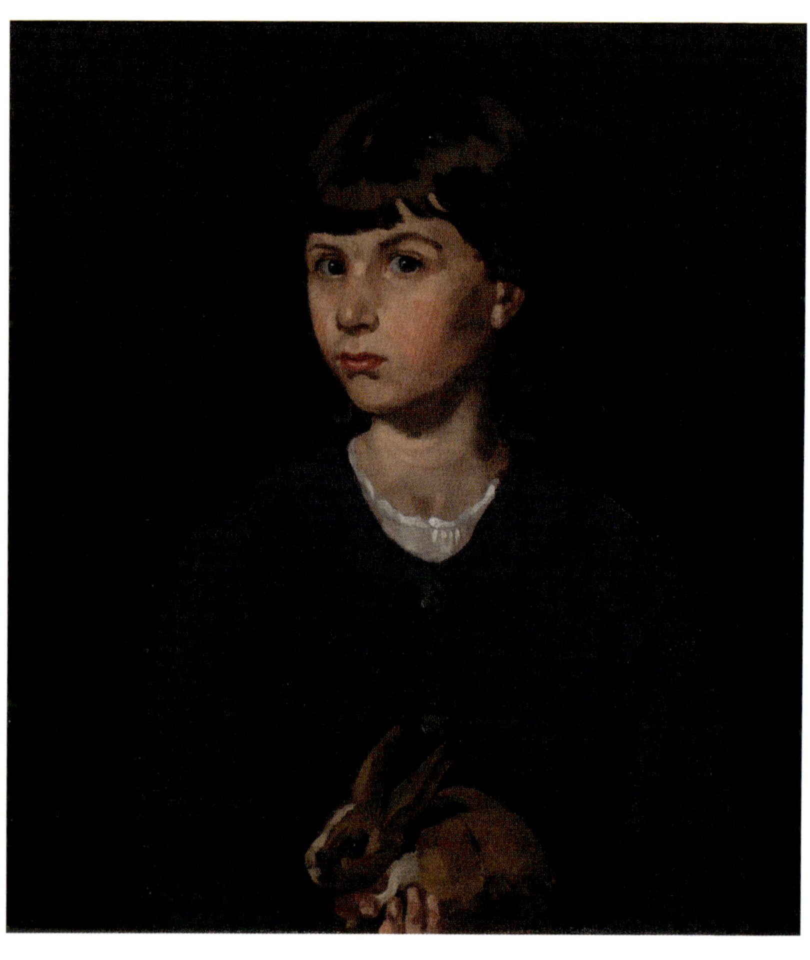

23. *Nancy with a Rabbit*, c.1910, oil on canvas

field. And much later, describing her silver wedding anniversary to Ben in 1917, she says that 'things just got right in time, and here I am once more forgetting everything and believing in people again, don't mention this please.'[77]

Still, in 1914, 'marital difficulties'[78] contributed to William accepting an invitation from Lutyens to travel to India for six months, where the architect, deep in plans for New Delhi, arranged for his friend to paint the Viceroy, Lord Hardinge. The Grange was sold, and Mabel moved temporarily to London before leasing a house for herself and the children by the sea at Harlech.

Wales

'Before motor traffic reached the North Welsh coast, Harlech was a very quiet place and little known,' wrote the poet Robert Graves, whose parents built a large house there in the 1890s, and would now be Mabel's neighbours. 'One hardly noticed the passage of the seasons there. The wind always blew across the stunted grass, the black streams always ran cold and clear, over black stones.'[79]

The Nicholsons' new house, Llys Bach – it means little courtroom – was a way outside Harlech on a steep hill, the driveway so difficult to conquer that William renamed the house 'slip back'. Graves first caught sight of 17-year-old Nancy there, about to leave for a party in a bandit costume. The meeting, followed by a second and a third in London, led to their engagement. He liked her 'child's heart', he wrote to Siegfried Sassoon[80], a quality he attributed to having a happy childhood to look back on. 'I liked all the family,' he writes in *Goodbye to All That*, 'particularly her mother … a beautiful, wayward Scotch-melancholy person.'[81]

Lutyens's daughters were equally taken with Mabel. In August 1916, Mabel and William stayed several weeks at Folly Farm, a country house in Berkshire that Lutyens was redesigning.

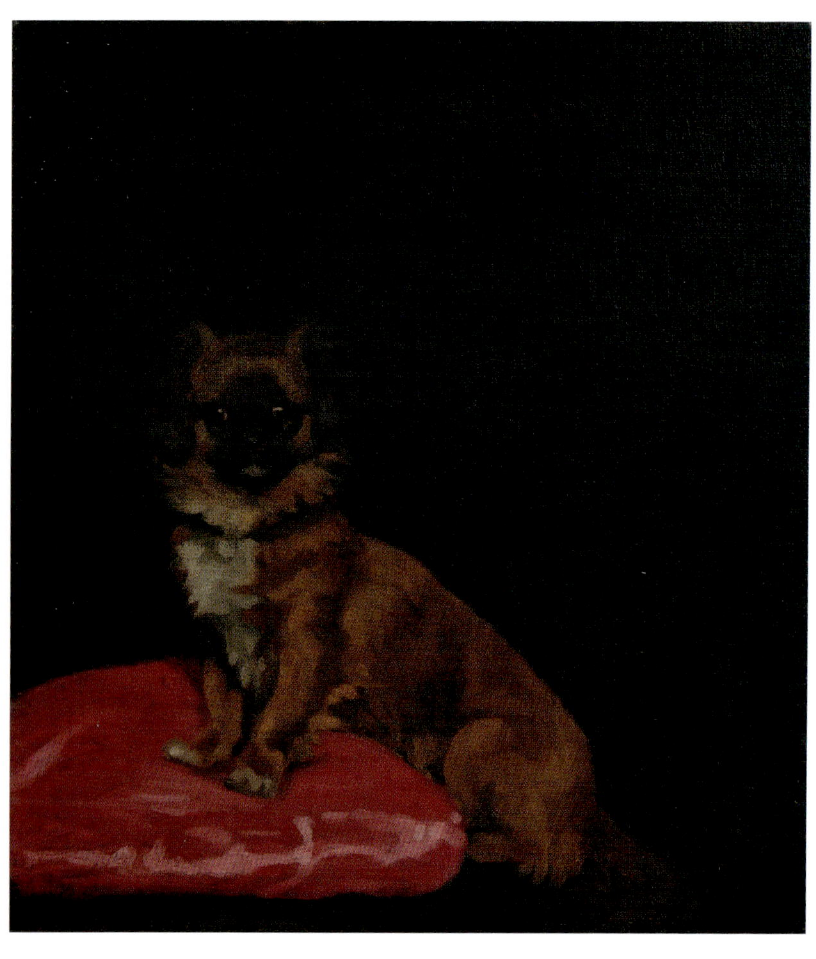

24. *Sneu-Ki (Pekingese)*, c.1912, oil on canvas (exhibited 1916)

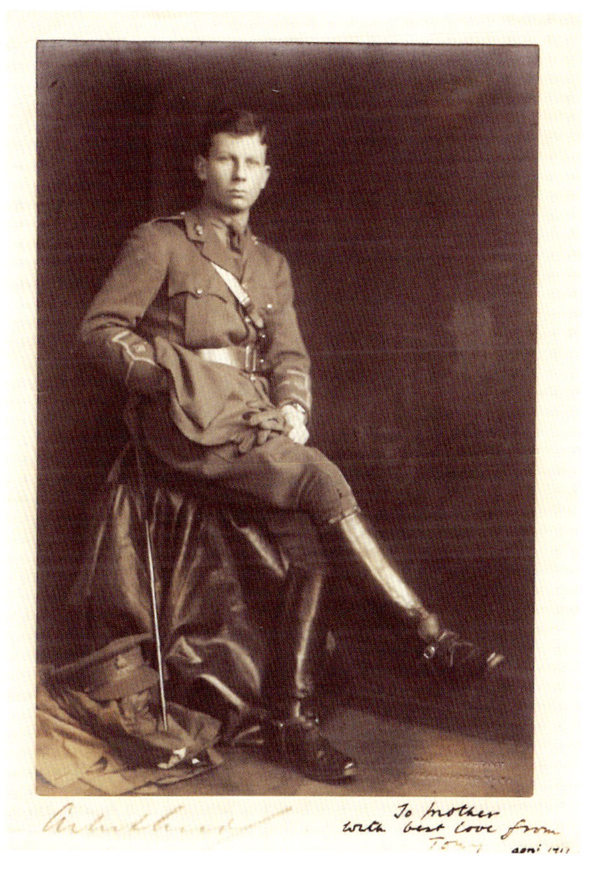

25. Portrait of Tony Nicholson in uniform by Malcolm Arbuthnot,
inscribed 'To Mother with love from Tony, April 1917'

last-minute leave unknowingly nursing the deadly strain of 'Spanish flu' that had been working its way through the trenches: three quarters of French and more than half of British troops had fallen ill. Mabel caught the overnight train to meet him in London and after a few days together they returned to Wales. A sequence of photographs taken in the garden at Maesyneuadd, the family and Edie squinting in the June sunshine, were almost certainly taken at this time (Fig. 26). Graves and Tony are in uniform, Nancy and Edie their breeches and smocks. Even the ordinarily elegant Mabel is in informal clothes. In one shot she holds Nancy's arm for support – was she already unwell? Another shows her arm threaded through Tony's. It's hard to see fully into the shadow cast by her hat, but she looks content; a little amazed at the physical presence of him.

Like any other influenza, 'The Spanish Lady' started with a sore throat and fever, but its particular sting was to ravage the lungs, filling them with so much fluid that the victim slowly suffocated. Tony was on a boat back to France when that began. Mabel had wanted so much to be with him in his final hours of leave that 'when the doctor came, she took quantities of aspirin, reduced her temperature and pretended to be all right,' wrote Graves. 'But she knew that the ghosts in the mirrors knew the truth. She died in London on 15 July [actually 13 July[91]] a few days later. Her chief solace, as she lay dying, was that Tony had got his leave prolonged on her account.'[92]

———

Graves wrote to Siegfried Sassoon a few days later, worrying about the effect the sudden death might have on their unborn baby, whom Mabel would now never meet. He and Nancy were staying at Maesyneuadd, which he – along with many other guests before and since – believed was riddled with ghosts.

26. Album page showing photographs of the family at Harlech, 1918

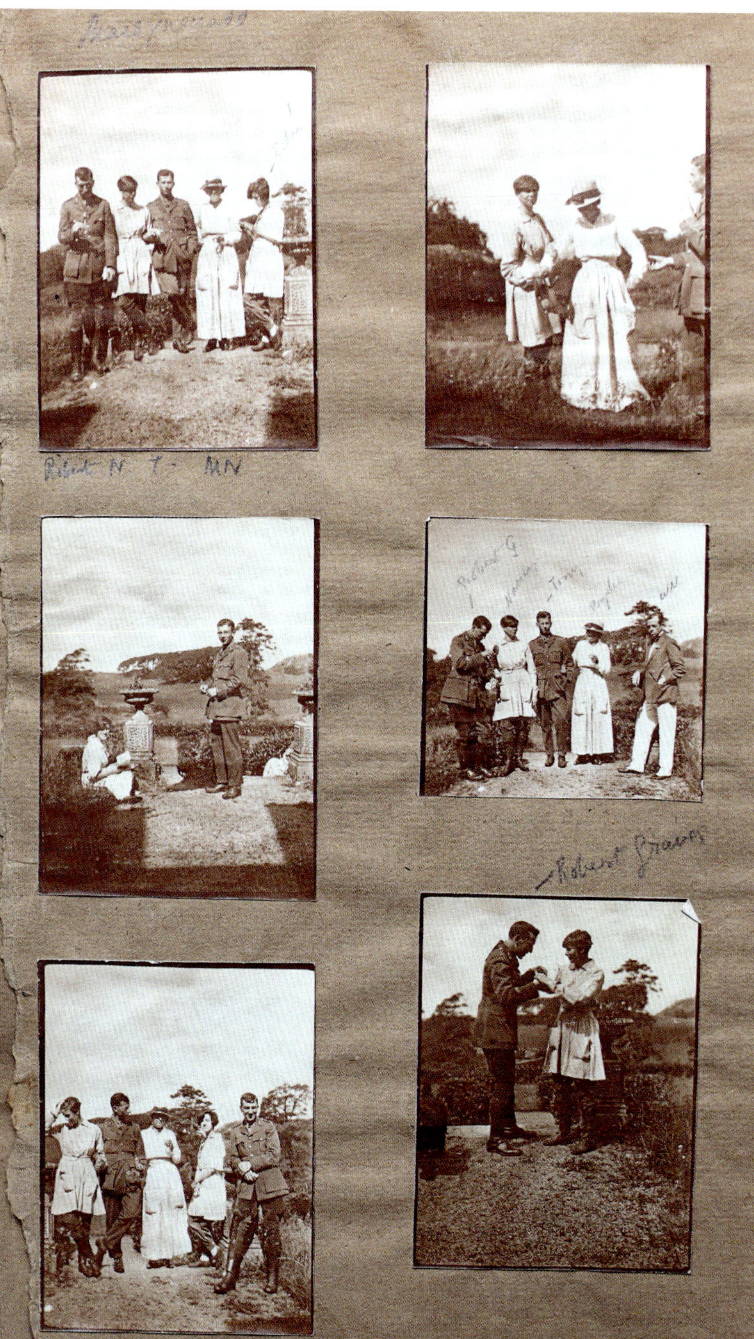
Harlech
Ricut N T - MN
Robert G   Nancy   Tony   Peyly   MN
Robert Graves

These included 'a little yellow dog that would appear on the lawn in the early morning to announce deaths. Nancy saw it through the window that time.'

Kit was dispatched to spend his summer holidays with the Lutyenses in Shropshire. 'I remember [William] joining us there one weekend,' recalled Ursula. 'I was haunted by the look of grief in his face, and he spent hours striding over the moors alone.' [93]

When, weeks later, Tony died of gunshot wounds in France – just a day after the German Chancellor requested 'the immediate conclusion of an armistice' – William took Ben and Nancy with him to break the news to Kit at school. 'Black times here with us,' he wrote to Reggie Turner the following day. 'I live entirely by habit now.' He was, he added, 'so thankful that Prydie did not open the telegram about Tony – it would certainly have killed her, and now they are really together I believe . . . She was such a darling. What a privilege to have lived 25 years with her. When do we meet again old friend? Come soon!'

In 1920, Ben and Nancy staged a memorial exhibition comprising 28 of Mabel's paintings at the Goupil Gallery, for which Graves wrote the catalogue note. Awarded a four-page feature in *Country Life* magazine, the exhibition was also favourably reviewed by *The Times* and *Sunday Times*, where the latter critic wrote that, among her cohort, 'Mrs Nicholson holds as distinct and honourable a rank as did Berthe Morisot among the French impressionists.' [94]

After this final blaze, however, Mabel blurred and then faded, becoming little more than a footnote in the stories of various Great Men, and altogether much underrated. By 1956, the art dealer Lillian Browse, whose book about William was for many years considered definitive, thought fit to describe Mabel as 'a somewhat inconsequent wife', [95] as if to muffle her, and the die was efficiently cast. Browse was William's dealer, but she was also a friend of Marguerite Steen.

William had been dead seven years by then, and could not refute it, nor Steen's two volumes of autobiography – *Looking*

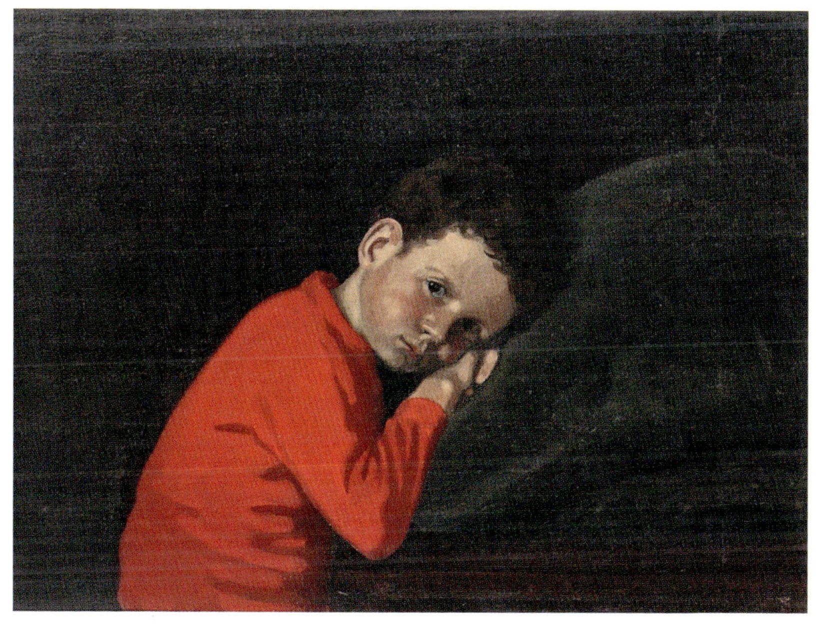

27. *The Red Jersey*, c.1912, oil on canvas

Glass (1966) and *Pier Glass* (1968) – in which she stated that William's first marriage 'left no happy memories behind'.[96] All their lives, however, Mabel's children fought to rescue and defend her; to resuscitate her as a painter – a good one – and a complex individual besides. 'Could we give some idea of mother's vital personality + contribution to my work?'[97] wrote Ben, outlining his origin story to John Summerson.

Steen came to believe that Mabel's ghost haunted her at Apple Tree Yard.[98] Since she also described meeting a reincarnated Ancient Egyptian princess we oughtn't to take the story *too* seriously, though inadvertently she hits on a truth. Mabel's paintings might look like realism, but they harbour enough of her memories, emotions and rare intuitions that it is as if she left a faint emanation of herself and her relationships with her children behind in the paint. To look at them is to be shuttled back to the moment of their making, in a Bloomsbury Square, on a bright day in Sussex.

Notes

1 Walter Sickert, 'Impressionism', quoted in Anna Gruetzner Robins (ed.), *Walter Sickert: The Complete Writings on Art* (Oxford 2000), p.60

2 Marguerite Steen, *Pier Glass*, (London 1968), p.29

3 Ben Nicholson, 'Memoirs: WN', *London Magazine*, June 1967

4 Letter to John Summerson, Jan 1944, Tate Archive

5 Letter to Herbert Read, Sep 1944

6 Letter to Ben Nicholson, 27 March 1914, Tate Archive

7 I am grateful to Sophie Bowness for drawing this to my attention

8 Article in *The Woman's Leader*, May 1920

9 Letter to John Summerson, Jan 1944

10 Steen, *William Nicholson*, (London 1943), p.41

11 Letter to James Pryde's biographer, Derek Hudson, 1948

12 Minutes of the Merchant Maiden Hospital (renamed Edinburgh Ladies College 1889)

13 Steen, *William Nicholson*, (cited note 10), p.34

14 Mabel Nicholson's posthumous exhibition catalogue at Goupil Gallery, 1920.

15 I am grateful to Patricia Reed for drawing this to my attention

16 Herkomer, *My School and My Gospel*, (New York 1908), p.207-8

17 Gordon Craig, *Index to the Story of My Days*, (Cambridge 1981), p.147

18 See for instance William Nicholson catalogue raisonné, (London 2011), p.57

19 Steen, *William Nicholson*, (cited note 10), p.68

20 Arcades Ambo, 'The Beggarstaff Brothers at Home', *The Idler*, Jan 1896

21 Craig, *Index to the Story of my Days*, (cited note 17), p.147

22 Steen, *Pier Glass*, (cited note 2), p.48

23 Craig, *An Index to the Story of my Days*, (cited note 17), p.177

24 Letter to Derek Hudson, 1948, quoted in *William Nicholson – Painter*, (ed), Andrew Nicholson, (London 1996), p.56

25 Mabel Nicholson to Ben Nicholson, Tate Archive

26 I am grateful to Tim Nicholson for drawing this to my attention

27 Robert Graves, *The Woman's Leader*, (cited note 8)

28 Steen, *William Nicholson*, (cited note 10), p.87

29 Steen, *William Nicholson*, (cited note 10), p.77

30 Steen, *William Nicholson*, (cited note 10), p.78

31 Ben Nicholson, *London Magazine*, (cited note 3)

32 *The Burlington Magazine*, vol.83, no.485, August 1943, pp.201–5

33 'Ben Nicholson: The Life & Opinions of an English Modern', *The Sunday Times*, 28 April 1963

34 1906 was also the year suffragette Sylvia Pankhurst [Modern Women
   Artists #1] went to prison for the first time. Earlier that year she led the
   Women's Social and Political Union's move from Manchester to Clements
   Inn in Holborn – a mile from Mecklenburgh Square

35 Steen, *William Nicholson*, (cited note 10), p. 109

36 Edith Craig, 'The Pioneer Player Reports', 1911–1915, Ellen Terry Memorial
   Museum, Smallhythe, undated. Quoted Kerry Powell (ed.), in *The Cambridge
   Companion to Victorian and Edwardian Theatre*, p.245.

37 Letter to Reggie Turner, 26 Nov, 1907

38 Letter to John Summerson, (cited note 4)

39 *The Sunday Times*, (cited note 33)

40 Letter to Hartley Ramsden, Feb 1943, Tate

41 Letter to John Summerson, (cited note 4)

42 Stephen Calloway, *Twentieth Century Decoration*, (London 1988), p.105

43 Paul Nash, *Vogue*, 1935, quoted in *William Nicholson – Painter*, (ed.),
   Andrew Nicholson, (cited note 24), p.91

44 Osbert Sitwell, *Great Morning*, (London 1948), p.235

45 Anne Helmreich and Ysanne Holt, 'Marketing Bohemia: The Chenil Gallery
   in Chelsea', 1905-1926, *Oxford Art Journal*, Vol. 33, No. 1 (2010), p.47

46 Nicholson, *London Magazine*, (cited note 3)

47 For the 1967 William Nicholson exhibition at Marlborough Gallery, London

48 Sold, Whyte's June 2022

49 Nicholson, *London Magazine*, (cited note 3)

50 Nicholson, *London Magazine*, (cited note 3)

51 Steen, *William Nicholson*, (cited note 10), p.106

52 musee-orsay.fr

53 Kenneth McConkey, *The Edwardians: The golden years before the war*,
   exhib catalogue for The Fine Art Society, London, 7–23 December 2011, p.29

54 The Nicholsons owned the Mecklenburgh Square house from 1906–1911

55 Sir Hugh Lane and Ruth Shine Papers, National Library of Ireland

56 Letter to Ben, 1908, Tate Archive

57 *Country Life* magazine, 18 April 1920

58 Letter to Moritz and Bertha Rothenstein, 13 January 1899, Tate Archive TAM
   50/4

59 Steen, *William Nicholson*, (cited note 10), p.86

60 Letter to Bacon postmarked 7pm Oct 14 1909, quoted in *William Nicholson
   – Painter*, (cited note 24), p 103

61 Letter to Bacon, November 1910, in *William Nicholson – Painter*,
   (cited note 24), p 106

62 Paul Nash, *Vogue*, 1935, (cited note 24), p.91

63 Steen, *William Nicholson*, (cited note 10), p.86

64 He abandoned the theme after the works failed to sell at his one-man show
   that November. See William Nicholson Catalogue Raisonné, p.104

65 Sitwell, (cited note 44)

66 *The Times*, 5 December 1910, p.14

67 Anne Helmreich and Ysanne Holt, (cited note 45), p.50

68 Untraced

69 The Beerbohm Collection at Merton College, Oxford

70 bankofengland.co.uk

71 *Zinnias and a Lustre Bowl* and *Evening in the Studio*, both 1912

72 Letter to Summerson, (cited note 4)

73 Letter 28 August 1911, *Max & Will*, ed. Mary M Lago & Karl Beckson, (London 1975), p.87

74 Sarah Ruhl, '100 Essays I Don't Have Time to Write', quoted in Julie Phillips' *The Baby on the Fire Escape*, (London 2022), p.11

75 Steen, *William Nicholson* (cited note 10), p.114

76 Letter, May 1910, from Mecklenburgh Square, Beerbohm Archive, Merton College, Oxford

77 Letter to Ben, 4 May 1917, Tate Archive

78 Catalogue raisonné (cited note 18), p.265

79 Robert Graves, *Goodbye To All That*, archive.org

80 20 November 1917

81 Graves, (cited note 79)

82 Mary Lutyens, *To Be Young*, (London 1959), p.42

83 9 Vale Avenue, a house in Chelsea the Nicholsons leased 1916-1917

84 Unpublished article, in *William Nicholson – Painter*, (cited note 24), p.143-146

85 Letter postmarked Omaha + Chelsea, 5.15pm 14 Dec 1917, quoted in *William Nicholson – Painter* (cited note 24), p.156

86 Letter to Ben 26 March, 1918, Tate Archive

87 31 December 1917

88 24 January 1918

89 4 May 1918

90 See William's 1918 painting *Lady in Grey* (Madame × as 'Megan' in Tân-y-Bryn) and the 1916 photograph of Mabel holding the family dog Bingo, taken by Ben outside Llys Bach.

91 Mabel Nicholson was cremated at Golders Green Crematorium on July 15

92 Graves, (cited note 79)

93 Unpublished article, quoted in *William Nicholson – Painter*, (cited note 24), p.145

94 *The Sunday Times*, 18 April 1920

95 Lillian Browse, *William Nicholson* (London 1956), p.10

96 Steen, *Pier Glass*, (cited note 2), p.29

97 Letter to John Summerson, (cited note 4)

98 Steen, *Looking Glass*, (London 1966), p.188-9

Image credits

1. Photograph of Mabel with Ben c.1896. Bushey Museum and Art Gallery (on loan from the collection of Nicholas Gibbs)
2. Possibly *Columbine*, exhibited 1911 (untraced), oil on canvas. Private collection. Photo: Stuart Walker
3. Photograph of students at Herkomer's School of Art, Bushey, late 1880s, from an album belonging to James Pryde. Bushey Museum and Art Gallery (on loan from the collection of Nicholas Gibbs)
4. William Nicholson, *Lady in Yellow (Mabel Nicholson)*, 1893, oil on canvas, 73 × 62.5 cm. Private collection, courtesy of Daniel Katz gallery
5. William Nicholson, *Portrait of Mabel Nicholson*, 1897, pencil and watercolour on card, 16.1 × 13.2 cm. National Galleries of Scotland, (presented by Mr and Mrs Samuel Graves, 2008)
6. Photograph of Mabel at Ben's school sports day, c.1901, with her face scratched out. Private collection. Photo: Clara Molden
7. Photograph of Ben with Cosmo Gordon Lennox, William Nicholson and Max Beerbohm, Dieppe, 1903. Private collection. Photo: Clara Molden
8. *Ben in the Feather Bonnet*, c.1908, oil on canvas, 65 × 55.5 cm. Pallant House Gallery, Chichester (on loan from a private collection, 2009)
9. Ben Nicholson, *1936 (white relief)*, 1936, oil on pencil on carved board, 54.6 × 70.5 cm. Pallant House Gallery, Chichester (on loan from a private collection, 2015) © Angela Verren Taunt. All rights reserved, DACS 2024
10. William Orpen, *A Bloomsbury Family*, 1907, oil on canvas, 86.5 × 91.5 cm. National Galleries of Scotland (presented by the Scottish Modern Arts Association, 1964)
11. *Kit as a Child with Harlequin Clothes*, c.1905, oil on canvas, 72 × 85 cm. Private collection. Photo: © The Fine Art Society Ltd
12. *The Harlequin*, c.1910, oil on canvas, 101.8 × 64.3 cm. Tate (presented by Timothy Nicholson 1982) Photo: Tate
13. *Ben Nicholson*, c. 1910-1914, oil on canvas, 76.2 × 63.5 cm. National Portrait Gallery. Photo: © National Portrait Gallery, London
14. *The Grange*, 1911, oil on canvas, 91.50 × 72.50 cm. National Galleries of Scotland (long loan in 1992)
15. Photograph of Kit with the model of HMS Pandora in the garden of The Grange, c. 1911/12. Private collection. Photo: Clara Molden
16. *Family Group*, c.1911, oil on canvas, 169.5 × 147.9 cm. Tate (presented by Timothy Nicholson 1991). Photo: Tate
17. *Kit in the Glass with Nancy and Sammy*, exhibited 1912 (untraced) showing MN in the mirror. Private collection. Photo: Stuart Walker

18. Possibly *The Pink Dress*, exhibited 1915 (untraced). Private collection. Photo: Stuart Walker
19. *Kit on the Platform*, c.1915 (untraced), showing WN on the left and MN in the mirror. Private collection. Photo: Walker
20. *William Nicholson*, c.1911/12, oil on canvas, 91.5 × 81.5 cm. Private collection
21. *Ernesto (Portuguese Boy)*, 1913, oil on canvas, 59.5 × 54.5 cm. Pallant House Gallery, Chichester (on loan from a private collection, 2013)
22. *A Portuguese Girl*, 1913, oil on canvas, 76.3 × 64 cm. Pallant House Gallery, Chichester (on loan from a private collection, 2013). Photo: Jonathan Bassett
23. *Nancy with a Rabbit*, c.1910, oil on canvas, 58.5 × 53.5 cm. Private Collection, courtesy of Patrick Bourne & Co.
24. *Sneu-Ki (Pekingese)*, c.1912 (exhibited 1916), oil on canvas. Pallant House Gallery, Chichester (on loan from a private collection, 2013)
25. Photographic portrait of Tony Nicholson in uniform by Malcolm Arbuthnot, inscribed 'To Mother with love from Tony, April 1917'. Private Collection
26. Album page showing photographs of the family at Harlech, 1918. Private Collection. Photo: Clara Molden
27. *The Red Jersey*, c.1912, oil on canvas, 55.5 × 74.1 cm. Aberdeen Art Gallery. Photo: © Aberdeen City Council (Archives, Gallery & Museums Collection)

About the author

Lucy Davies writes for publications including *The Times*, *BBC Culture*, *The Telegraph*, *The Times Literary Supplement*, *World of Interiors* and the *V&A Magazine*. She is the former visual arts editor of *The Telegraph* and the author of books on Women Painters and British Art. She lives in London.

Acknowledgements

In writing about Mabel Nicholson, I've benefited enormously from the generosity and expertise of her family, especially Sophie and Lady Sarah Bowness, Tim and Catherine Nicholson, Louisa Creed, Jovan Nicholson and Desmond Banks. I'm also grateful to Patricia Reed and Cordelia Bourne who have patiently answered questions, and to the librarians and archivists at the Fine Art Society, Tate Britain, the V&A, London Library, Bushey Museum, the Harry Ransom Center, Merton College Oxford and Golders Green Crematorium.

Thank you to my comrades David Bomford and Chris Davidson and to the whole team at The Grange in Sussex – Mabel's former home. To Rottingdean Heritage for their assistance with images. To Iona McLaren who read an early draft of the book and whose comments improved it immeasurably, to Carrie, for always being in my corner and to Harriet Olsen who commissioned this book, for her enthusiasm and formative interventions. Finally, I wouldn't have set out on this path without the encouragement of the late Professor David Daniell, who taught me to find the story behind the story. This book is for him, and for M and W.

Index

Entries in *italics* refer to paintings unless indicated; the artist is Mabel Nicholson unless named. Family members are referred to in other entries by forename and initial (e.g. William N.). Pages in *italics* refer to photos or paintings.

Mabel Nicholson
By Lucy Davies
First Edition

First published in the United Kingdom in 2024 by Eiderdown Books
Eiderdownbooks.com

Series conceived and developed by Eiderdown Books
Text © Lucy Davies
Images © see Image credits

A CIP record for this book is available from the British Library.

ISBN: 978-1-916515-02-4

Copy-edited by Denny Einav
Indexed by Jan Worrall
Series design by Clare Skeats
Typeset by Clare Skeats in Lelo by Katharina Köhler

The Modern Women Artists logotype is set in Hesse Antiqua which was released in 2018 to mark the 100th birthday of Gudrun Zapf von Hesse. The forms of Hesse Antiqua are based on the metal punches that von Hesse created in 1947 while working as a bookbinder at the Bauer Type Foundry in Frankfurt.

Printed and bound by Latitude
Reprographics by ALTA

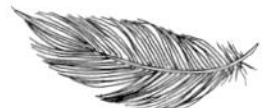